The Relief of Poverty 1834–1914

Prepared for
The Economic History Society by

MICHAEL E. ROSE

Lecturer in Economic History
at the University of Manchester

MACMILLAN

First edition 1972
Reprinted 1974

Published by
THE MACMILLAN PRESS LTD
London and Basingstoke
Associated companies in New York Dublin
Melbourne Johannesburg and Madras

SBN 333 11236 9

Printed in Great Britain by
THE ANCHOR PRESS LTD
Tiptree, Essex

Contents

Acknowledgements

I am grateful to the Passfield Trustees for permission to quote from the Passfield Papers. My thanks are due to my colleagues at Manchester University who have helped in any way in the production of this short study and particularly to Dr W. H. Chaloner for reading the preliminary draft and for his ever-welcome and valuable advice. I owe a particular debt of gratitude to the editor of this series, Professor M. W. Flinn, for his careful and critical reading of the manuscript and for his exemplary patience despite the numerous delays which occurred during its production. My typist, Mrs M. Gissop, worked speedily and accurately once the manuscript appeared. It is traditional for an author to thank his wife for her patience and sympathy. In this, if in nothing else, I am a fervent traditionalist.

M. E. R.

Editor's Preface

SO long as the study of economic history was confined to only a small group at a few universities, its literature was not prolific and its few specialists had no great problem in keeping abreast of the work of their colleagues. Even in the 1930s there were only two journals devoted exclusively to this field. But the high quality of the work of the economic historians during the inter-war period and the post-war growth in the study of the social sciences sparked off an immense expansion in the study of economic history after the Second World War. There was a great expansion of research and many new journals were launched, some specialising in branches of the subject like transport, business or agricultural history. Most significantly, economic history began to be studied as an aspect of history in its own right in schools. As a consequence, the examining boards began to offer papers in economic history at all levels, while textbooks specifically designed for the school market began to be published.

For those engaged in research and writing this period of rapid expansion of economic history studies has been an exciting, if rather breathless one. For the larger numbers, however, labouring in the outfield of the schools and colleges of further education, the excitement of the explosion of research has been tempered by frustration caused by its vast quantity and, frequently, its controversial character. Nor, it must be admitted, has the ability or willingness of the academic economic historians to generalise and summarise marched in step with their enthusiasm for research.

The greatest problems of interpretation and generalisation have tended to gather round a handful of principal themes in economic history. It is, indeed, a tribute to the sound sense of economic historians that they have continued to dedicate their energies, however inconclusively, to the solution of these key problems. The results of this activity, however, much of it stored away in a wide range of academic journals, have tended to remain inaccessible to many of those currently interested in the subject. Recognising the need for guidance through the burgeoning and confusing literature that has grown around these basic topics, the Economic History Society decided to launch this series of small books. The books are intended to serve as guides to current interpretations in important fields of economic history in which important advances have recently been made, or in which there has recently been some significant debate. Each book aims to survey recent work, to indicate the full scope of the particular problem as it has been opened up by recent scholarship, and to draw such conclusions as seem warranted, given the present state of knowledge and understanding. The authors will often be at pains to point out where, in their view, because of a lack of information or inadequate research, they believe it is premature to attempt to draw firm conclusions. While authors will not hesitate to review recent and older work critically, the books are not intended to serve as vehicles for their own specialist views : the aim is to provide a balanced summary rather than an exposition of the author's own viewpoint. Each book will include a descriptive bibliography.

In this way the series aims to give all those interested in economic history at a serious level access to recent scholarship in some major fields. Above all, the aim is to help the reader to draw his own conclusions, and to guide him in the selection of further reading as a means to this end, rather than to present him with a set of pre-packaged conclusions.

M. W. FLINN
Editor

1 Introduction

ONE of the major problems involved in any study of poverty, even at the present day, is that of definition. Poverty might be said to consist of a lack of the basic necessities of life, but the things thought to be necessary for a minimum standard of civilised life vary widely from society to society and from age to age. As Adam Smith recognised, 'by necessities I understand not only the commodities which are indispensably necessary for the support of life, but whatever the custom of the country renders it indecent for creditable people, even of the lowest order, to be without'.[1] In the past few years, the truth of Adam Smith's comment has been increasingly recognised as social scientists have begun to criticise the concept of a poverty line, of taking a point on the income scale which is thought to be the minimum amount necessary for healthy physiological subsistence and then arguing that all those living below this point are in poverty.[2] It is not the purpose of this study to enter into the debate on the definition and extent of poverty in modern British society, but it is perhaps valuable to remember, before entering into a critical examination of the relief of poverty in the nineteenth century, that our knowledge of the subject at the present day is by no means complete and in some areas has not moved far from the concepts laid down by social investigators in the period under discussion. In this way we shall guard against what Professor Titmuss has called 'the placid conventional textbook account of the historical romance of "Welfare Statism" '.[3]

British society in the nineteenth century was poor by modern

[1] A. Smith, *The Wealth of Nations*, book v, chap. 2, part ii, quoted in A. B. Atkinson, *Poverty in Britain and the Reform of Social Security* (1969) p. 17.

[2] P. Townsend, 'Measuring Poverty', *British Journal of Sociology* (1954), and 'The Meaning of Poverty', ibid. (1962); S. Mencher, 'The Problem of Measuring Poverty', ibid. (1967).

[3] R. M. Titmuss, Foreword to B. B. Gilbert, *The Evolution of National Insurance in Great Britain: The Origins of the Welfare State* (1966) p. 8.

6

standards. The net national income per head at 1900 prices has been estimated at £18 in 1855 and £42 in 1900, as compared to £57 in 1938.[4] Certainly most members of the working class were likely to experience poverty at some period of their lives. Even the highest-paid artisan might find himself in a period of trade depression to be 'out of collar', unable to get work even if willing and anxious to do so. At such times he would be forced to rely on the earnings of his children, assistance from friends, and credit from local tradesmen in order to keep house together until things 'took a turn'. 'This', commented such an artisan in 1868, 'is about as settled a kind of life as the great body of working men can hope to attain.'[5] For a large proportion of the working population indeed such a level was unattainable, and their experience of poverty was likely to be a far more frequent, if not a permanent one.

The nineteenth century had inherited the attitude that such a state of affairs was right and proper. Poverty had been regarded by many writers as a necessary element in society, since only by feeling its pinch could the labouring poor be inspired to work. Thus it was not poverty but pauperism or destitution which was regarded as a social problem.[6] Faced with this problem, many early Victorians adopted an attitude which combined fatalism, 'the poor ye have always with you', and moralism: destitution was the result of individual weakness of character. 'So far from rags and filth being the indications of poverty, they are in the large majority of cases, signs of gin drinking, carelessness and recklessness', preached *Fraser's Magazine* in 1849.[7] Such cases if congregated together in large numbers seemed to constitute a social menace.

> Tis'n them as 'as munny as breaks into 'ouses an' steals,
> Them as 'as coats to their backs an' taakes their regular
>   meals.

[4] B. R. Mitchell and P. Deane, *Abstract of British Historical Statistics* (1962) pp. 367–8 (figures for the U.K.).
[5] 'A Journeyman Engineer' [Thomas Wright], *The Great Unwashed* (1868).
[6] See Patrick Colquhoun, *On Destitution* (1806) pp. 7–9.
[7] 'Work and Wages', *Fraser's Magazine* (Nov 1849).

Noa, but it's them as niver knaws wheer a meal's to be
    'ad.
Taake my word for it, Sammy, the poor in a loomp is
    bad,

remarked Tennyson's northern farmer,[8] and there were many in
Victorian England who shared his opinion, particularly when
they saw or read of the vagrants and beggars who crowded into
the cheap lodging-houses of London and other rapidly expanding
cities. Such characters, it was felt, could not be left to starve, if
only because such treatment might drive them to acts of despera-
tion, but equally the taint of pauperism which they carried with
them must not be allowed to infect the honest working man and
destroy his character.

It was thinking of this sort which provided the impetus for
the Poor Law Amendment Act of 1834. The fear that the so-
called 'Speenhamland system' of poor relief allowances in aid of
wages was undermining the independence of the agricultural
labourer seemed to strengthen the case for a system of poor relief
in which outdoor payments to the able-bodied would be abolished.
All the members of this class who applied for relief would be
offered maintenance in a workhouse in which their lives would
be regulated and made less comfortable than those of their
fellows who chose to stay outside and fend for themselves. This
scheme of 'less eligibility' had the attraction of being a self-acting
test of destitution. Those who were genuinely in dire need would
accept the workhouse rather than starvation. Those who were
not in such straits would prefer to remain independent and thus
avoid contracting the morally wasting disease of pauperism. As
Dr Marshall has shown in a previous contribution to this series,
the allegedly demoralising effects of the Old Poor Law were
wildly exaggerated by the propagandists of the New Poor Law of
1834.[9] Nevertheless, so great was the fear of pauperism that the
ruling classes were ready to believe the exaggerations contained in
the Report of the Royal Commission on the Poor Laws. They
were even prepared to accept, although with some modifications,

[8] Alfred, Lord Tennyson, 'The Northern Farmer – New Style', in
Collected Poems, Everyman ed., vol. II : *1857–69,* p. 262.
[9] J. D. Marshall, *The Old Poor Law, 1795–1834* (1968).

the new system of poor law administration which it recommended, despite the fact that this contained a far greater degree of bureaucratic centralisation than would have been acceptable to them under normal circumstances. The New Poor Law was seen as a final solution to the problem of pauperism which would work wonders for the moral character of the working man.

The New Poor Law did not provide any such solution, nor, despite the claims of the new central authority for poor relief, the three Poor Law Commissioners of Somerset House, can it be shown to have done very much to improve either the material or the moral condition of the working classes. On the other hand, it was less inhumane in its operation than some of its opponents alleged. If wages of agricultural labourers did not rise dramatically in areas where the allowance system was prohibited, neither were the skins of old pauper women who died in the workhouse used to provide chair covers for the Poor Law Commissioners or bindings for parish registers as *Blackwood's Magazine* half seriously alleged they would be in 1838.[10]

Such stories were not untypical of the propaganda produced by the opposition which greeted the introduction of the New Poor Law. This reached its climax after 1837 when the Poor Law Commission sent its assistant commissioners into the industrial areas of northern England to form Unions and inaugurate the new relief system. In Lancashire and in the West Riding of

[10] 'A New Scheme for Maintaining the Poor', *Blackwood's Magazine* (Apr 1838). A High Tory periodical, *Blackwood's* had consistently opposed all attempts to reform the Old Poor Law which it saw as a fundamental part of the old paternalist order of society. Stories of the cruelties practised in New Poor Law workhouses were common in the late 1830s and formed a staple part of the propaganda of the Anti-Poor Law campaign. On investigation they often proved to be false or at least considerably exaggerated. The celebrated Andover scandal of 1846 was the result more of the failure of the Poor Law Commission to enforce its authority than of the rigid and doctrinaire administration of the new system. See D. Roberts, 'How Cruel Was the Victorian Poor Law?', *Historical Journal,* vi (1963); U. Henriques, 'How Cruel Was the Victorian Poor Law?', ibid., xi (1968). An interesting collection of Anti-Poor Law propaganda can be found in G. R. Wythen Baxter, *The Book of Bastilles* (1841).

Yorkshire, an organised Anti-Poor Law movement appeared. Opponents of the New Poor Law like Richard Oastler, John Fielden and Joseph Rayner Stephens attacked the Act and its administrators from the platform and in the Press. They painted lurid pictures of the treatment accorded to applicants for relief in the workhouses of southern England where the Act was already in operation.

With the onset of trade depression in 1837, industrial workers, particularly those in decaying handicraft trades, were feeling the pinch of poverty. They feared that were the New Poor Law to be introduced, they would no longer be given outdoor relief to maintain them until trade conditions improved but would be confined with their families in a grim workhouse, a New Poor Law 'Bastille'. They reacted strongly to this prospect and riots greeted the attempted introduction of the new system at Bradford in 1837 and at Dewsbury and Todmorden in 1838. This unrest gave impetus to the embryonic Chartist movement in northern England, and the Home Secretary urged the Poor Law Commission to exercise caution and delay in their extension of the New Poor Law to the area.[11]

It was not only working men, the prospective recipients of poor relief, who were in revolt against the New Poor Law. Those who had administered the old system of relief – parish overseers, magistrates, members of select vestries – were outraged at the prospect of interference by the new central authority. They felt that the old system under their guidance had worked in both an economic and a humane way in northern parishes. Furthermore they argued with some justice that the idea of relieving the able-bodied poor only in well-regulated workhouses was irrelevant to the problems of industrial parishes in which there were few able-bodied paupers when trade was good, and more than even the largest workhouse could accommodate in times of economic depression. Thus they obstructed the implementation of the New Poor Law, perhaps the best example of this being at Huddersfield where the new board of guardians refused to proceed to the election of a clerk for the new Union, and the local magistrates as

[11] N. C. Edsall, *The Anti-Poor Law Movement, 1834–44* (1971); M. E. Rose, 'The Anti-Poor Law Agitation', in J. T. Ward (ed.), *Popular Movements c. 1830–1850* (1970).

ex officio members of the board would do little or nothing to overcome the obstinacy of their elected colleagues.[12]

In the face of this dangerous amalgam of working- and middle-class resistance, the Poor Law Commission was forced to tread warily. Boards of guardians and poor law Unions were at first established in the northern countries merely for the purpose of carrying out the provisions of the Registration Act of 1836. Even when they were persuaded to take over responsibility for poor relief from the parish authorities, they were allowed to continue to give relief in the old way without any ruling as to the withdrawal of outdoor relief from the able-bodied. Having made these concessions, the central authority found it difficult to withdraw them. The workhouse test was never enforced in the industrialised Unions of Lancashire and the West Riding, and even the regulation that able-bodied male applicants for relief be subjected to some form of task work was evaded or ignored by boards of guardians who demanded that they be given full discretion to relieve their poor as they thought fit.[13] Outdoor relief to the able-bodied continued, even in some cases in the form of allowances in aid of inadequate earnings.[14] The Poor Law of 1834 provided an important administrative model for future generations, but the workings of this model were often profoundly disappointing to the advocates of 'less eligibility' as a final solution to the problem of pauperism.[15]

[12] C. Driver, *Tory Radical: The Life of Richard Oastler* (1946) chaps 25–7.

[13] Rhodes Boyson, 'The New Poor Law in North East Lancashire, 1834–71', *Transactions of Lancashire and Cheshire Antiquarian Society,* LXX (1960); M. E. Rose, 'The New Poor Law in an Industrial Area', in R. M. Hartwell (ed.), *The Industrial Revolution (1970).* In the North-east, the introduction of the New Poor Law seems to have had a smoother passage. See N. McCord, 'The Implementation of the 1834 Poor Law Amendment Act on Tyneside', *International Review of Social History,* XIV (1969).

[14] M. E. Rose, 'The Allowance System under the New Poor Law', *Economic History Review,* XIX (1966).

[15] O. R. McGregor, despite his condemnation of the 'paralysing fatalities of the principles of 1834', admits that the Act 'created an administrative revolution and thus provided a model for future developments'. O. R. McGregor, 'Social Research and Social Policy

Whatever their importance in administrative history, the Report of the Royal Commission on the Poor Laws, and the Act which followed hard on its heels, contained weaknesses which severely limited their usefulness in dealing with poverty, or even with pauperism, in the second half of the nineteenth century. In the first place, the Royal Commission had concentrated too much of its attention upon a single problem, that of the able-bodied unemployed, particularly in rural areas, who it feared were being demoralised by ill-conceived grants of outdoor relief. It paid too little regard to the problems of those who were pauperised because of physical or mental ill health, old age or loss of parents, although these probably constituted by far the largest proportion of those on relief. The important and complex problem of settlement received only cursory treatment in the Report and was only modified in a few minor details by the Act, and the vital question of rating and the finance of poor relief was dealt with in an equally cavalier fashion. These were questions which were to harass poor law administrators and social reformers for the next hundred years. Secondly, the reformers of 1834 focused their attention upon the problem of rural poverty, and produced the machinery to deal with it. Yet the problem of the future was to be the far more difficult one of urban, industrial poverty.

The poor law proved to be ill adapted for dealing with poverty, and thus was increasingly ignored as a device for social reform. It is the aim of this study to follow this development, to see the extent to which the oversimplified early nineteenth-century view of poverty was broken down by investigation of the causes of poverty, and by changing attitudes towards it, a process which led to the introduction of new methods of treating poverty.

in the Nineteenth Century', *British Journal of Sociology*, VIII (1957) 148.

2 The Extent of Poverty

AN obvious preliminary to any study of poverty in the nineteenth century is to determine approximately how many people were in poverty during this period. Yet this is a question which is impossible to answer with any degree of accuracy even with regard to those who, having applied for poor relief, were officially recorded as paupers. This seems curious in view of the massive collection of statistical tables which filled the appendices to the annual reports of the central authority for poor relief, the Poor Law Commission, after 1847 the Poor Law Board and, after 1871, the Local Government Board. 'English poor law statistics surpass those of all other countries both in their scope and in the time over which they extend', wrote an eminent German judge in a study of the English poor law system. Yet he followed up these words of praise with a detailed critique of the deficiencies of the statistics, which the Webbs echoed in their final volume on English poor law history.[16]

One difficulty lay in the fact that the central authority, particularly in its early years, placed more emphasis on the collection of statistics relating to poor relief expenditure than to those recording the number of persons relieved. The Webbs held that before 1849 the aggregate number of persons relieved could be safely estimated only from the tables of relief expenditure. The Poor Law Commission published returns of the number of paupers relieved in the last quarter of the administrative year, the quarter ending at Lady Day which covered the period from 25 December to 25 March. Not only was this the period in which the numbers relieved would be at a maximum, but there was considerable uncertainty as to whether a person relieved on

[16] P. F. Aschrott, *The English Poor Law System Past and Present*, 2nd ed. (1902) Appendix II, pp. 326–51. For other critical accounts of English poor law statistics, see S. and B. Webb, *English Local Government*, vol. IX : *English Poor Law History*, part 2, vol. 2 (reprinted 1963) Appendix II; Lord George Hamilton, 'A Statistical Survey of the Problems of Pauperism', *Journal of the Royal Statistical Society*, LXXIV (1910–11).

three occasions during this period would count as one pauper or as three. After 1848, the Poor Law Board, and later the Local Government Board, asked for figures of those relieved on two days of the year only, 1 January and 1 July. It was argued that pauperism would be at its height on the former date, and at its lowest ebb on the latter. Thus the average of the two would give the approximate average number of paupers relieved on each day of the year. But if the tendency of the quarterly return was to overstate the number of paupers, the tendency of the daily return was to understate them. A count of all paupers relieved during 1907 produced a figure two and a half times greater than that calculated from the average of those relieved on 1 January and 1 July of that year.

Even if the margin of error contained in these figures was not serious enough to affect their approximate accuracy as a measure of the total number of paupers relieved in any one year, serious difficulties arose if any attempt was made to use them for a more subtle analysis of pauperism. No guide was given as to the length of time during which paupers were relieved, as to whether they were chronic cases relieved on 1 January and for the rest of the year, or temporary cases relieved only on 1 January or for one or two weeks after that date. The practice of dividing those relieved into 'able-bodied' and 'non-able-bodied' did not give much help in this direction, since the term 'able-bodied pauper' was never clearly defined. Most Unions regarded all paupers between the ages of sixteen and seventy as being 'able-bodied' if they were not permanently incapacitated. Thus a young man of twenty admitted to the workhouse infirmary with a broken leg might be listed as able-bodied, whilst an old man of seventy-five, even if still capable of work, would be registered as 'non-able-bodied'.

Another factor tending to complicate poor relief statistics was the phenomenon of 'constructive' pauperism. If the head of the family received relief, the whole family were registered as paupers. If a child, or other legal dependant, received relief, then the head of the family was also recorded as being in receipt of relief. Nor was the distinction between those relieved in the workhouse, indoor paupers, and those relieved in their own homes, outdoor paupers, always as clear-cut as might have been expected. As the

14

century wore on, an increasing number of paupers were relieved in institutions not directly under the control of the boards of guardians, schools for the deaf or the blind for example. Such paupers were recorded as being in receipt of outdoor relief despite the fact that they were being cared for in institutions.

Despite the difficulties of making any very sophisticated analysis of the problem of pauperism on the basis of the official poor law statistics, the overall trends which they showed undoubtedly gave satisfaction to many poor law administrators. Thus the number of paupers on relief fell from an estimated 1·26 million, 8·8 per cent of the population in 1834, to 1 million, 5·7 per cent of the population, in 1850. By 1860 the figure was 845,000, 4·3 per cent of the population. The next decade showed no significant decrease and by 1870 there were again just over 1 million on relief, 4·6 per cent of the population. By 1880, however, the total had fallen to 808,000, only just over 3 per cent of the population, and by 1900 only 2·5 per cent of the population were estimated to be in receipt of relief.[17] After this, the proportion tended to increase slightly, giving rise to fears about a recrudescence of pauperism, especially as the cost of poor relief was increasing more rapidly than were the numbers relieved.[18] Nevertheless, judging by the statistics of the central authority for poor relief, it might seem that improved poor law administration in conjunction with a rise in the standard of living of the working classes had reduced poverty to a problem of relatively minor proportions.[19]

The surveys of working-class life carried out by Charles Booth in the East End of London from 1887 and by Seebohm Rowntree in York in 1899 showed this argument to be fallacious. Booth in the first volume of his massive survey of East London showed that over 30 per cent of the population had an income which was inadequate for their support.[20] Seebohm Rowntree in

[17] See below, Appendix A.
[18] See below, Appendices B and C.
[19] For an expression of this point of view, see Robert Giffen, 'The Progress of the Working Classes in the Last Half Century', in *Essays in Finance,* 2nd ed. (1887).
[20] Charles Booth, *Life and Labour of the People in London,* 17 vols (1902–4). The first volume in the series appeared in 1889.

his more advanced survey of York conducted ten years later found 28 per cent of the population to be in this condition, thus proving that Booth's results were no freak.[21] Yet according to the statistics of the Local Government Board only 2·8 per cent of the population of England and Wales were in receipt of poor relief and thus officially classified as paupers in 1889, and only 2·6 per cent in 1899. If the poor law statistics were no very sensitive record of pauperism, they were totally incompetent as a measure of poverty.

Booth, Rowntree and a number of other investigators of working-class life who followed them in the decade before the outbreak of the First World War[22] showed that a significant proportion of the population of England and Wales were living in poverty without having recourse to poor relief. Small earnings were supplemented by receipts of money, food or clothing from charitable organisations. Booth found a widow in the East End who attended every mission hall and every mothers' meeting she could : 'this brings her soup three or four times a week and sometimes a loaf of bread, and so the poor woman keeps her little room and the children with bread'.[23] In hard times, local shopkeepers gave credit and frequent recourse was made to the pawnshop. A speaker at the Social Science Association's conference in 1861 claimed that printers in Glasgow were producing pawn tickets at the rate of 10 to 15 million a year.[24] 'Sir, we don't live;

[21] B. S. Rowntree, *Poverty: A Study of Town Life* (1901). On Booth's and Rowntree's methods and the effects of their surveys, see below, pp. 27–30.

[22] See, e.g., Lady F. Bell, *At the Works* (1907); Mrs P. Reeves, *Round About a Pound a Week,* 2nd ed. (1914); Maude Davies, *Life in an English Village* (1909); B. S. Rowntree, *How the Labourer Lives* (1913); A. L. Bowley and A. R. Burnett-Hurst, *Livelihood and Poverty* (1915). Several of these observers confirmed Booth's and Rowntree's estimate that about 30 per cent of their sample were living in poverty. Thus in Corsley (Wiltshire), Maude Davies estimated that 65 of the 220 households in the parish fell below the poverty line.

[23] A. Fried and R. Elman, *Charles Booth's London* (1969) p. 63.

[24] D. Macrae, 'Pawnbroking', *Transactions of the National Association for the Promotion of Social Science* (1861) p. 621.

we only linger', an agricultural labourer's wife told an investigator in the 1890s who inquired how she and her family managed to live on 10s. a week.[25] Yet for many working men, such misery was preferable to official poor relief which they regarded with fear and contempt. Henry Mayhew pointed out that in 1848, 1·87 million people were estimated to be in receipt of poor relief, but 2·25 million, about 14 per cent of the population, had no gainful occupation. Even the vagrant, the lowest and most despised of the nineteenth century's poor, shunned the poor law. Mayhew reckoned that whilst 849 tramps on average were relieved every night in London's workhouses, a further 2,431 sought shelter in cheap lodging-houses, preferring their dirt and discomfort to the hard discipline of a workhouse casual ward.[26] Even had official poor law statistics been more accurately compiled, they could not have recorded anything like the true extent of nineteenth-century poverty which must have included at least one-third of the population.

3 The Causes of Poverty

OF all the causes of poverty in the nineteenth century, the most prominent was poverty resulting from the receipt of inadequate or irregular earnings. Even the limited statistics of the Poor Law Commission showed that in the early 1840s between 16 and 20 per cent of adult able-bodied persons in receipt of poor relief were being aided because of 'insufficient wages'.[27] Lord George Hamilton, in an analysis of poor law statistics published in 1910, showed that rates of pauperism were highest in occupations where casual labour was predominant.[28] Poor relief in aid of low

[25] F. Verinder, 'The Agricultural Labourer', in F. W. Galton (ed.), *Workers on their Industries* (1896) p. 164.
[26] H. Mayhew, *London Labour and the London Poor* (new impression, 1967) III 398.
[27] Rose, op. cit. (1966) p. 608.
[28] Hamilton, op. cit., p. 11.

earnings, particularly to women workers, was given by many boards of guardians until the 1870s when the Local Government Board launched a campaign against the practice. Nevertheless it seems to have survived this onslaught in some Unions. Maude Davies found that in Corsley 'several women in receipt of poor relief add a little to their incomes by gloving'.[29] Booth and Rowntree showed low and irregular earnings to be a major cause of the poverty they discovered. Booth found that 55 per cent of the poverty in his lowest classes, A and B, and 68 per cent of that in classes C and D was the result of casual or irregular work, which he condemned as being 'the most serious trial the people of London suffer'.[30] Rowntree revealed that 52 per cent of the primary poverty in York was the result of low wages.[31]

A common contributory cause of poverty for low-wage earners was a large family. Rowntree thought this to be the cause of 22 per cent of the primary poverty in York, and showed in his description of the poverty cycle how a young married couple were dragged further below the poverty line as the size of their family increased.[32]

Maude Davies noted the high percentage of children in families affected by poverty in Corsley, and A. L. Bowley in 1912 estimated that nearly half of those aged under fourteen in Reading were living below the poverty line.[33] Child poverty was a common feature of nineteenth-century England.

Sickness, particularly when it struck down the chief breadwinner of the family, was frequently a cause of poverty. As far as poor relief was concerned, the Poor Law Commission's statistics for the period 1842–6 showed that between 40 and 50 per cent of those on outdoor relief were relieved on account of sickness or accident, and the Royal Commission of 1905–9 revealed that 30

[29] Davies, *Life in an English Village,* p. 127.

[30] T. S. and M. B. Simey, *Charles Booth, Social Scientist* (1960) p. 182.

[31] Rowntree, *Poverty,* pp. 120–1. For a discussion of the term 'primary poverty', see below, p. 29.

[32] Ibid., pp. 120–1, 137.

[33] Davies, *Life in an English Village,* chap. 12; Bowley and Burnett-Hurst, *Livelihood and Poverty,* p. 43.

[34] Poor Law Commission, *Annual Reports, 1843–7* (hereafter

per cent of paupers were receiving medical treatment.[34] Where the sickness proved fatal, poverty was even more likely to be the lot of the deceased's dependants. Widows with dependent children constituted a high proportion of poor law relief cases in the nineteenth century. According to the Poor Law Commission which listed them separately in its early statistical tables, they usually constituted between 17 and 20 per cent of all adult able-bodied paupers on outdoor relief between 1840 and 1846.[35] The meagre doles of poor relief granted to them were usually inadequate for maintenance and had to be eked out by earnings from charring or domestic work, and by grants from private charity. 'Widows or deserted women and their families brought a large contingent into the ranks of those suffering from great poverty,' remarked Booth, who discovered that 18 per cent of the very poor in Shoreditch were members of families with female heads.[36] Rowntree estimated that 23 per cent of primary poverty was the result of the death, incapacity or unemployment of the chief wage-earner.[37]

The aged were often to be reckoned among those in poverty. The Poor Law Commission's annual reports showed that over half the adult paupers on outdoor relief were aged and infirm.[38] Not until 1890, however, was there any statistical breakdown of paupers by age. Lord George Hamilton, analysing such a return for March 1906, showed that whilst only 3 in every 1,000 persons aged fifteen to twenty-five were in receipt of poor relief, 163 in

---

abbreviated to P.L.C.); Webb, *English Local Government*, IX 514. Figures for the Lady Day quarter of each year.

[35] P.L.C., *Annual Reports, 1841–7*. Figures for the Lady Day quarter.

[36] Simey, *Charles Booth*, p. 182.

[37] Rowntree, *Poverty*, pp. 120–1.

[38] The figures for the quarter ending at Lady Day were as follows :

	Able-bodied	Aged and infirm
1840	203,060	262,879
1841	231,069	268,750
1842	269,446	269,946
1843	309,589	288,748
1844	282,234	294,582
1845	281,032	302,694
1846	247,171	295,366

Source: P.L.C., *Annual Reports, 1841–7.*

every 1,000 aged between sixty-five and seventy-five were on relief, and 276 of those aged from seventy-five to eighty-five.[39] Booth, analysing the relief books of the Poplar and Stepney Unions in a paper which he presented to the Statistical Society in 1892, found old age to be the most frequent single cause of pauperism in the district, accounting as it did for about one-third of all cases.[40] The debate on old-age pensions which waxed continuous from the 1890s on produced further evidence of the extent of poverty among the old.

Low earnings, irregular employment, large families, sickness, widowhood and old age – these rather than intemperance or idleness were the root causes of poverty in the nineteenth century. It was during the eighty years which form the chronological boundaries of this pamphlet that these causes were isolated and publicised. In this period new levels of poverty were discovered showing clearly that the official statistics of pauperism revealed only the tip of the iceberg, and that comfortable assumptions based on the notion that poverty would melt away in the warm climate of economic prosperity must be considerably modified. It is to this process of discovery that we must now turn.

4 *The Investigation of Poverty*

THE deficiency of statistics on poverty and in particular the gap between the official estimates of pauperism and those of poverty made by Booth, Rowntree and other social investigators, the tendency to oversimplify the causes of poverty and to ascribe to weakness of character destitution which was the result of an ill-organised labour market or an ill-drained slum, seem to confirm our worst suspicions of the Victorian treatment of poverty. Until the last decade of the century when private social investigation

[39] Hamilton, op. cit., p. 7.
[40] C. Booth, 'Enumeration and Classification of Paupers and State Pensions for the Aged', *Journal of the Statistical Society*, LIV (1891) 610, 637.

began to stir the national social conscience, it would seem that the typical attitude to poverty was either one of unconcern and complacency, or of a concern that took the form of a moralising and patronising charity. Either middle-class mid-Victorians felt with Mr Podsnap that there was 'not a country in the world, sir, where so noble a provision is made for the poor as in this country', or like Mrs Pardiggle they burst into the homes of the poor leaving broth, tracts and good advice until the objects of their compassion demanded 'an end of being drawed like a badger'. Behind these comfortable middle-class assumptions lay the harsh realities of the Victorian poor law, symbolised by the grim work-house in which little Oliver Twist suffered.

Undoubtedly the idea of 'less eligibility' as the best means of making the poor fend for themselves profoundly influenced social policy in Victorian England. In the early 1870s the Local Government Board and its inspectorate launched a campaign against outdoor relief in an attempt to get the poor law back to the 'principles of 1834'.[41] Up to the outbreak of the First World War and beyond, there remained those who believed that the systems advocated in the Report of 1834 provided the best and safest solution to the problem of poverty.[42] *Laissez-faire,* although never systematically applied in the field of social policy, was strongly entrenched as an attitude of mind. Self-help and independence were praised as virtues, and those who failed to exhibit these characteristics were regarded with a degree of contempt. Such attitudes were by no means confined to the wealthier classes. The skilled artisan, the 'labour aristocrat' of Victorian England, looked upon fellow workers of a lower grade with condescension.

[41] Webb, *English Local Government,* viii 364–95.

[42] Charles Booth, for example, retained a strong belief in individualism until his death in 1916. His advocacy of old-age pensions was based on the belief that if the aged poor could be removed from the poor law, it would be possible to abolish outdoor relief entirely. Simey, *Charles Booth,* p. 161.

In 1921 the Ministry of Health reminded boards of guardians that outdoor relief given to the unemployed 'should of necessity be calculated on a lower scale than the earnings of the independent workman who is maintaining himself by his labour'. See M. E. Rose, *The English Poor Law, 1780–1930* (1971) p. 295.

He reacted with horror to the idea of being treated as a casual labourer or a pauper in hard times.

> We're mixt wi th' stondin paupers, too,
> Ut winno wark when wark's t' be had,
> A scurvy, fawnin, whoinin crew –
> It's hard to clem, bo that's as bad,

wrote Joseph Ramsbottom, expressing the feeling of many of his fellow cotton operatives about their treatment at the time of the Lancashire cotton famine.[43]

Yet despite their belief in self-help, the privileged classes could not entirely shut up the bowels of compassion. Evangelical religion and concern for social stability pulled in the opposite direction from political economy. 'We really can't quite button up our pockets, invest our spare cash as prudently as may be, and say to the poor man, "Starve for it serves you right", . . . If a pauper cannot but envy us, it is desirable that he should hate us as little as possible', argued a contributor to the *Saturday Review*.[44] One result of this was the massive Victorian investment and involvement in charitable activity. Such activity, as David Owen and Brian Harrison have shown, was often of more benefit to the giver than to the recipient, providing as it did an outlet for the energies of bored and frustrated middle-class women and countless opportunities for social climbing.[45]

Yet although Podsnaps and Pardiggles undoubtedly existed in the mid-nineteenth century, it would be unfair to condemn the Victorian attitude to the poor as one compounded of ignorance, contempt, fear and uneasy condescension. The Victorians were driven to investigate poverty, especially urban poverty, and thus provide the foundations upon which later Victorian and Edwardian social investigators and reformers could build. Outstanding in this role was Henry Mayhew, whose investigations of the

[43] Joseph Ramsbottom, 'The Operative's Lament', quoted in R. A. Arnold, *History of the Cotton Famine* (1864) p. 148. 'clem'=starve.

[44] 'Charity and Pauperism', *Saturday Review*, 16 Jan 1869.

[45] D. Owen, *English Philanthropy, 1660–1960* (1965) chap. 17; B. Harrison, 'Philanthropy and the Victorians', *Victorian Studies*, IX (1965–6).

London poor for the *Morning Chronicle* in 1849 led on to the publication of his four massive volumes on *London Labour and the London Poor*. Mayhew, for long regarded as a mere cataloguer of the quaint in the London street scene, has been rescued by Edward Thompson from what he has referred to, in another context, as 'the massive condescension of posterity'.[46] Mayhew, he points out, was engaged in a serious study of Victorian poverty. He counted, listed and generalised before going on to interview in depth, describing his work as 'the first commission of enquiry into the state of the people undertaken by a private individual', and believing that he could 'contribute some new facts concerning the physics and economy of vice and crime generally'.[47] He showed that much destitution was due to sheer insufficiency of wages, that accidental circumstances like three wet days could bring 30,000 people in London to the brink of starvation. He challenged the notion that the poor were poor because they were drunken or idle, or that philanthropy could ease their inevitable sufferings and teach them patience. 'For a brief period, Mayhew pierced this protective shell of Podsnappery. He discovered not poverty but a middle-class consciousness of poverty. The shell healed quickly.'[48]

Such a comment perhaps overrates the uniqueness of Henry Mayhew. The shell did not heal so quickly, as thinking middle-class people, particularly in the growing industrial towns, became increasingly conscious of the poverty which surrounded them and increasingly dissatisfied with existing methods of treating it. In the mid-nineteenth century 'there emerged a new generation of reformers, practical and hard-headed but still interested in humanity who saw problems realistically and sought efficient and accurate means of pursuing their aims'.[49] Many of

[46] E. P. Thompson, 'The Political Education of Henry Mayhew', *Victorian Studies*, xi (1967–8).

[47] H. Mayhew, *London Labour and the London Poor* (1967 reissue) vol. i : *London Street Folk*, Preface, p. iii; vol. iv : *Those That Will Not Work*, p. 1.

[48] Thompson, op. cit., p. 43.

[49] Ruth Hodgkinson, 'Social Medicine and the Growth of Statistical Information', in F. N. L. Poynter (ed.), *Medicine and Science in the 1860s* (1970) p. 184.

these reformers were members of local statistical societies which provided a focus for the collection, analysis and discussion of statistics relating to social problems. This local interest was reflected nationally in the activities of the Statistical Society, whose *Journal* 'provided a quantitative commentary on the trends of social change and the social incidence and running costs of expansive industrialism'.[50]

The Statistical Society encouraged the formation in 1857 of the National Association for the Promotion of Social Science, whose annual sessions frequently devoted themselves to the discussion of problems of poor relief. Speakers criticised existing methods of treatment and atiitudes to the poor, and pleaded for more informed and accurate approaches to the problem. Philanthropists like William Rathbone in Liverpool stressed the need not only to arouse in the wealthy a sense of their social obligations but also to work out sound methods by which these could be expressed.[51] A society like the Workhouse Visiting Society, founded by Louisa Twining in 1858, did not confine its activites to distributing tracts, goodies and words of comfort to workhouse inmates, but collected information on workhouse conditions and used this to agitate for an improvement in the treatment of the sick or aged poor.

Although the activities of Mrs Twining aroused the hostility of poor law authorities both central and local, poor law officials played their part in the mid-nineteenth-century movement for a more informed approach to poverty. Despite the heavy burden of routine administrative work to which they were subjected, the assistant commissioners of the Poor Law Commission and the inspectors of the Poor Law Board investigated and prepared detailed reports on many aspects of the life of the poorer classes. J. P. Kay's reports on the education of pauper children in the 1830s, and Edward Smith's investigations into the dietary habits of the poorer classes in the 1860s, are outstanding but not exceptional examples of this process.[52] At the local level, the poor law

[50] H. L. Beales, *The Making of Social Policy in the Nineteenth Century*, Hobhouse Memorial Lecture (1946) p. 17.

[51] M. B. Simey, *Charitable Effort in Liverpool in the Nineteenth Century* (1951).

[52] Poor Law Commission, *Report on the Training of Pauper Child-*

24

medical officer often played a vital role in collecting information and arousing consciences on the subject of the treatment of the poor. Not only did the medical officer obtain an intimate knowledge of the conditions under which the poor lived, he was often a young doctor anxious to improve his status and conditions of work in the face of a board of guardians which aimed at obtaining his services at the cheapest possible rate. Expressing their grievances individually or through bodies like the Poor Law Medical Officers' Association and periodicals like the *Lancet*, the medical officers put forward an informed case for improved treatment both for themselves and for their pauper patients. By the 1860s the profession had raised their status considerably and gave weighty support to the national campaign for better treatment of sick paupers in workhouses which commenced with the *Lancet's* investigation and exposure of the state of sick wards in a number of London workhouses in 1865.[53]

The culmination of these developments towards a greater and more accurate knowledge of the poor might be seen in the formation of the Charity Organisation Society in 1869. With its stern insistence on individualism and self-help, its rejection of state aid except in a minor role and its distinction between the deserving and the undeserving poor, it might seem to epitomise all that was worst in the Victorian attitude to the poor. Canon Samuel Barnett, a founder member of the society, who finally broke with it in 1895, described its members as 'clothing themselves in the dirty rags of their own self-righteousness'. Yet despite these attitudes, most historians of social policy agree that the Charity Organisation Society had a valuable contribution to make to the development of British social welfare. Distinguishing between the deserving and undeserving, and deciding upon the best means of restoring the deserving poor to independence, involved patient, detailed investigation of the circumstances of the case.

---

ren (1841) Appendices II–VI; Dr E. Smith, *Report to the Poor Law Board on Dietaries of Inmates of Workhouses* (1866).

[53] Ruth Hodgkinson, *The Origins of the National Health Service: The Medical Services of the New Poor Law, 1834–71* (1967); J. E. O'Neill, 'Finding a Policy for the Sick Poor', *Victorian Studies,* VII (1963–4).

In their advocacy of proper casework and investigation, the C.O.S. were not entering an entirely virgin field. Thomas Chalmers in Glasgow in the 1820s, the Metropolitan Visiting and Relief Association in London in the 1840s, the German town of Elberfeld in the 1850s, and Liverpool's Central Relief Society in the 1860s had all made use of the system of visiting the poor in order to assess the nature of their needs. The C.O.S. drew on this experience in its insistence on the proper training of social workers, and established its own training scheme in 1896. 'Charity', wrote its secretary C. S. Loch, 'requires a social discipline; it works through sympathy, it depends on science'.[54] Not only did the C.O.S. reject indiscriminate almsgiving, it also opposed the ignorant, condescending attitudes which often went with it. The society's founders were concerned at what they saw as a widening gulf between rich and poor, and advocated greater contact between the classes, a contact which should not be entered into in a spirit of patronising interference. 'Well to do strangers', the society warned, 'should no more knock at the door of a working man without some distinct object or introduction than they should at the door of one in their own rank of life'.[55]

Once contact had been established and a proper investigation of the needs of the case carried out, the society insisted that no expense be spared in giving the help best designed to restore the recipient to independence. Mrs Bosanquet rejected the idea of distributing as much money to as many people as possible as old-fashioned, and urged its replacement by another attitude to charity, that of meeting each specific need and difficulty as it arose with an appropriate and adequate remedy.[56]

In its stern insistence on self-reliant individualism as the only formula for social progress, the C.O.S. was to find itself by the turn of the century increasingly in opposition to a new generation of social reformers who believed that in increasing collectivist control of society and the economy lay the best hope for the solution of the poverty problem. It is, however, essential to recognise the

[54] Quoted in C. L. Mowat, *The Charity Organisation Society, 1869–1913* (1961) p. 71.

[55] Helen Bosanquet, *Social Work in London, 1869–1912* (1914) p. 56.

[56] Idem, *Rich and Poor* (1898) chap. 10.

very positive contribution which the society made towards the attack on nineteenth-century poverty, particularly through its insistence on careful, dispassionate investigation. Even at the height of their disagreement with the C.O.S. members of the Royal Commission on the Poor Laws of 1905–9, the Webbs paid public tribute to the society's work. 'We do not, in this generation', they wrote, 'adequately realise how great an advance in thought was expressed in the very name of the society'.[57]

The mid-Victorians laid the foundations on which late Victorian and Edwardian social reformers could build. Charles Booth, the wealthy Liverpool shipowner, whose investigations into the condition of the poor in the East End of London between 1887 and 1903 constituted a vitally important new departure in the field of social investigation, was an individualist of the C.O.S. school. He was annoyed by sensational accounts of urban poverty which were appearing in the early 1880s in pamphlets like *The Bitter Cry of Outcast London* or in newspapers like the *Pall Mall Gazette*. Such alleged revelations, Booth felt, provided sustenance for the emergent socialist societies whose doctrines he abhorred. Yet what irritated him most about these accounts was less the political use to which they could be put than the scientific misuse which they involved. To Booth's rational, scientific mind, allegations such as that made in the *Pall Mall Gazette* in March 1886 that 25 per cent of London's population was in distress had little factual basis and were calculated to appeal to emotion rather than reason.[58]

In order to demonstrate that human society could be described and analysed by the use of statistics and scientific observation, Booth with his seven voluntary helpers began his survey of the life of the East End's working class. To the statistical framework provided by the official Census Reports, Booth added information on living and working conditions provided by school board visitors and by his own inquiries and those of his assistants. Even before the publication of the first volume of his *Life and Labour*

[57] S. and B. Webb, 'The Sphere of Voluntary Agencies in the Prevention of Destitution', N.C.P.D., *Leaflets and Pamphlets* (1911–12) B.M. 8285, dd. 36.
[58] See D. Rubinstein, 'Booth and Hyndman', *Bulletin of the Society for the Study of Labour History* (spring 1968).

of the People in London in 1889, Booth had already demonstra-
ted in two papers to the Statistical Society that the *Pall Mall
Gazette* was in error, and that not a quarter but a third of the
East End's population was in want.

Booth's importance, however, lay less in his revelations as to
the extent and causes of poverty, invaluable though these were,
than in the method by which he approached and measured
poverty. His concept of the 'poverty line' has been described by
Professor Simey as 'perhaps his most striking single contribution
to the social sciences'.[59] The idea of taking some minimum income
level, in Booth's case 18*s*. to 21*s*. a week for an average family
of man, wife and three children, below which it was impossible
to provide even the nutritional elements necessary for healthy
physical existence, provided an objective measure of poverty
shorn of any moral or emotional assumptions.[60] A poverty line
drawn across society at a certain level showed very clearly the
extent of poverty in relation to the rest of the community. Booth
and the social investigators who followed him examined poverty in
the context of the whole society. What they were surveying was
poverty, the faults in the lower parts of the social edifice, and
not just pauperism, the human rubble at the base of the structure.

Of those who followed Booth's pioneering work, the most
important was Benjamin Seebohm Rowntree. Son of the wealthy
York cocoa manufacturer, Rowntree possessed an interest in
statistics together with a deep social concern springing naturally
from his Quaker education and beliefs. Booth's work fascinated
him and he decided to apply similar techniques to a survey of his

[59] Simey, *Charles Booth,* p. 88.
[60] Although Booth retained some moralistic preconceptions about
the poor which occasionally show through in his work : 'a woman
with two grown up daughters all looking hardened in sin'; 'the old
woman is very clean, sober, industrious, honest . . . a rare specimen
in this neighbourhood'. Fried and Elman, *Charles Booth's London,*
pp. 77, 80. Thus Booth was willing to suggest harsh treatment for
the very lowest classes of the poor to remove them from the labour
market. Class B could be sent to labour colonies leaving class A, the
small semi-criminal group, to be harried out of existence. See John
Brown, 'Charles Booth and the Labour Colonies, 1889–1905',
Economic History Review, xxi (1968).

home town, a task which he carried out in 1899, aided by one paid investigator and a few volunteer helpers. The results published in 1901 under the title *Poverty: A Study of Town Life* confirmed, as has been seen, the findings of Charles Booth a decade earlier.[61]

Yet Rowntree did far more than merely dot the i's and cross the t's of the Booth survey. Taking Booth's methods as his starting-point, he developed and considerably improved his technique. His poverty line was drawn more precisely and accurately than Booth's had been. Rowntree's minimum was fixed at the very exact figure of 21s. 8d. a week for man, wife and three children, a level arrived at only after detailed investigation of physiological data bearing on the nutritional needs of the human body. These investigations enabled Rowntree to make a distinction between primary poverty, resulting from an income insufficient to provide even the bare necessities of physical well-being, and secondary poverty, resulting from the unwise expenditure of income which, given highly disciplined budgeting, could have kept the family above the poverty line in physical terms. The concept of secondary poverty 'enriched the notion of poverty by indicating that living in a state of poverty was not entirely a matter of income'.[62]

Another original contribution which Rowntree made to the scientific study of poverty was his idea of the poverty cycle. By means of this device, Rowntree was able to show that an individual might rise above the poverty line only to fall below it again at a later stage in his life. The child of a poor family might struggle out of poverty once he began work and contributed to the family earnings, only to fall below it again if he married and produced a family. He might again rise out of poverty once his children began to earn, and then might well end his days in poverty once the children left home and he became too old for anything but ill-paid and infrequent light work. The poverty cycle showed poverty to be a dynamic and not merely a static concept.

Without having to resort to sensationalism or dogmatism,

[61] See above, p. 16.
[62] Mencher, op. cit., p. 7.

Charles Booth and Seebohm Rowntree produced not only the facts regarding the extent and causes of poverty in late Victorian England but also the tools for its further investigation. These tools were taken up by other social investigators before the First World War, perhaps the most detailed use of them being made by Professor Arthur Bowley who carried out a survey of four widely differing towns in 1912–13.[63]

It is important, however, not to see the work of Booth and Rowntree in isolation without noticing the vital changes in social thinking and attitudes which occurred during the period in which their investigations were being carried out. Their findings fell on the ears of a receptive generation, particularly the younger generation of late nineteenth-century England. As Professor Simey has shown, Booth was moving with the tide of opinion in his day.[64] One direction in which this tide was flowing was against the prevalent mid-Victorian ideal of self-help and individualism. Social reformers were increasingly willing to countenance a more positive role for the state in the making of social policy. Even Booth, convinced individualist though he was, advocated non-contributory state pensions for all aged citizens. 'We are part of a social system', said Seebohm Rowntree, 'and must play our part as part of a great whole and if we fail to play our part nobly the whole is marred'.[65] Sidney Webb, celebrating Lord Rosebery's escape from the tenets of Gladstonian individualist Liberalism, remarked, 'we have become aware, almost in a flash, that we are not merely individuals but members of a community, nay, citizens of the world'.[66]

The less confident climate of economic expectation in late nineteenth-century England, together with the growing realisation that economic growth had done little to reduce urban poverty, helped to bring this reaction against the ideas of *laissez-*

[63] Bowley and Burnett-Hurst, *Livelihood and Poverty*. The towns surveyed were Reading, Warrington, Northampton and Stanley (Co. Durham).

[64] Simey, *Charles Booth,* p. 9.

[65] Quoted in A. Briggs, *Social Thought and Social Action: A Study of the Work of Seebohm Rowntree, 1871–1954* (1961) p. 13.

[66] S. Webb, 'Lord Rosebery's Escape from Houndsditch', *Nineteenth Century,* L (1901) 369.

faire. The growth of socialism in the 1880s, particularly the moderate reformist socialism of the Fabian Society, founded in 1884, reflected this trend against individualism in social policy. Another important force pressing for greater state intervention in social problems was 'New Liberalism'. This challenge to the tenets of orthodox Gladstonian Liberalism drew much of its inspiration from the philosophical writing and teachings of the Oxford tutor and philosopher Thomas Hill Green, who died in 1882.[67] In his work, Green stressed the importance of 'positive freedom' in place of the merely 'negative freedom' of orthodox Liberalism. He pleaded the case of the weaker members of society who were 'being left to sink or swim in the stream of unrelenting competition'. 'So far as negative rights go – the rights to be let alone – they are admitted to membership of civil society, but the good things to which the pursuits of society are in fact directed turn out to be no good things for them', Green argued, and pointed out that more positive intervention by central and local government could create a climate in which every individual could realise his full potential.[68] Although himself retaining many of the ideals of individualistic Liberalism, Green's ethical concern for the poor, expressed both in his writing and teaching and in his practical work on the Oxford city council, inspired whether directly or indirectly a generation of social reformers. A group of these, J. A. Hobson, J. L. Hammond, L. T. Hobhouse, C. F. G. Masterman and others, centring around H. W. Massingham's weekly, the *Nation*, after 1906, constituted a small but intellectually formidable influence on the left of the Liberal Party.

The self-conscious imperialism of the late nineteenth century went along with socialism and New Liberalism in pointing the need for more positive state action to create an efficient nation, an imperial race fitted for a world role. As Bernard Semmel has demonstrated, imperialism and social reform went together.[69] Even before the shocks of the Boer War had drawn public

[67] See M. Richter, *The Politics of Conscience: T. H. Green and His Age* (1964).

[68] Ibid., p. 320.

[69] B. Semmel, *Imperialism and Social Reform* (1960) chap. iii. See also B. Porter, *Critics of Empire* (1968).

attention to the deficiencies of British military power, voices had been raised against an economic and social system which seemed to be producing a degenerate, sickly race in the slums of the great cities. Conservative and Liberal imperialists were drawn together with Fabian socialists in their demands for national efficiency, for organisation springing out of the chaos of *laissez-faire* capitalism.[70]

The declining faith in individualism was strongest among the younger generation. Young men and women from comfortable backgrounds experienced a sense of guilt and frustration at the sight of a mass of poverty existing at the heart of the wealthiest nation in the world. Their moral idealism was impatient with the traditional palliatives for social distress. 'They were conscious of something wrong underneath modern progress, they realised that free trade, reform bills, philanthropic activity and missions had made neither health nor wealth. They were drawn to do something for the poor', remarked Canon Samuel Barnett, one of the instigators of the Settlement Movement, which gave young university graduates the opportunity of dwelling and working among the poor of London's East End.[71] It was this impatience which drove Beatrice Potter from the social round of her upper-middle-class milieu to her 'industrious apprenticeship' under Charles Booth.[72] The young William Beveridge, inspired by his tutors at Balliol, T. H. Green's college, and intensely frustrated by legal work which 'does not go about slaying any dragons', became sub-warden of Toynbee Hall, Barnett's original settlement, and from there began his study of the problem of unemployment.[73] C. F. G. Masterman, dissatisfied even with the settlement ideal because of its overtones of patronising philanthropy, took a worker's flat in Camberwell in order to experience at first hand the life of the poor which he struggled to improve through his work as a poor law guardian, journalist and later as an M.P. and a junior member of the Liberal

[70] For an excellent portrayal of this ideal in fictional terms, see H. G. Wells, *The New Machiavelli* (1911).
[71] Canon S. A. Barnett, 'University Settlements' in W. Reason, *University and Social Settlements* (1898) p. 12.
[72] B. Webb, *My Apprenticeship* (1926).
[73] W. Beveridge, *Power and Influence* (1953) p. 13.

Government.[74] Beatrice Potter, Beveridge, Masterman and others like them believed that the remedy for the problems of poverty lay in radical social reconstruction based on careful investigation of the type pioneered by Booth and Rowntree.

It was not only youthful middle-class idealism which was instrumental in creating a climate favourable to the research of Booth and Rowntree. From the 1880s the pressure of an increasingly organised and articulate working class began to be felt. The Trafalgar Square riots of 1886 created widespread alarm among the wealthier classes and drew serious attention to the problem of unemployment.[75] The 'new unions' of the unskilled and semi-skilled brought the problems of the low-paid, casually employed worker into the public eye. The extension of the franchise in 1884, and the struggle for an independent working-class party in Parliament culminating in the formation of the Parliamentary Labour Party in 1906, may have made the existing political parties more sensitive to the issues of social reform. It should, however, be remembered that 40 per cent of adult males were still unenfranchised in 1911, and that the Labour Party was little more than a trade union pressure group in its early years. Perhaps more important in voicing the working-class demand for a new approach to poverty were those working men like Will Crooks and George Lansbury in Poplar who were gaining election to town councils and boards of poor law guardians, particularly after the abolition of the property qualification for membership in 1894. With their philosophy of 'decent treatment and hang the rates', they drew attention to the shortcomings of poor relief from the recipients' rather than the ratepayers' point of view. Thus at the same time as Booth and Rowntree were conducting their inquiries and publishing their findings, an increasingly organised and articulate working class was questioning the reasons for the existence of the poverty they were uncovering.

Booth, Rowntree and the social investigators who followed them revealed the extent and causes of poverty in late Victorian and Edwardian Britain. The causes of poverty, it seemed, could

[74] Lucy Masterman, *C. F. G. Masterman* (1939) p. 28.
[75] Gilbert, *The Evolution of National Insurance*, pp. 32–40.

33

be isolated like the causes of cholera or typhoid, and thus destroyed by social science just as bacilli could be destroyed by medical science. There was a growing feeling that radical cures must be found and implemented, a growing impatience with philanthropy and poor relief as mere palliatives, plasters for the sores of destitution, not cures for the disease of poverty. It should of course be stressed that such feelings were almost certainly those of a minority, albeit an intelligent, active, influential and vocal one. There were many who remained steadfast to their faith in self-help and individualism, and who were convinced that the plight of the poor was too often due to their failings in such matters as thrift, industry and temperance. The investigation of poverty exposed the weakness of these attitudes, and pointed to the need for a more constructive approach. 'The most conspicuous result of the general restatement of problems which has taken place within recent years', said R. H. Tawney in 1913, 'has been the diversion to questions of social organisation of much of the attention which, a generation ago, was spent on relief.'[76]

5 The Treatment of Poverty

THE increasing investigation of poverty in the second half of the nineteenth century and the changing attitudes towards the poor which were ever more apparent from the 1880s on, brought the two main nineteenth-century agencies for poor relief, private charity and the poor law system, under increasing scrutiny and criticism. The Charity Organisation Society cast a coldly critical eye over much of the charitable activity of Victorian England. They attacked indiscriminate almsgiving which failed to discover the needs of the recipient and which laid itself open to the incessant claims of the fraudulent. They criticised impertinent interference in the lives of the poor by well-meaning but ignorant philanthropists, particularly of the female variety. A part of their

[76] R. H. Tawney, *Poverty as an Industrial Problem,* Inaugural Lecture of the Ratan Tata Foundation (1913) p. 12.

work was devoted to the investigation and exposure of fraudulent charities, with even such a respectable institution as Dr Barnardo's Homes attracting their attention at one stage in its career.

But whatever the shortcomings of private charity, the public relief system of the poor law attracted even stronger criticism. As has been seen, an uneasy compromise emerged after the Act of 1834. New Unions were established, new workhouses built, and in some areas the idea of 'less eligibility' was put into practice, at least with regard to the able-bodied poor. Yet, given the considerable freedom within which the local boards of guardians were allowed to operate by the central authority, many elements of the old system remained. This arrangement made for flexibility and enabled the new system to be adapted to differing local circumstances.

Slackness of central control did not, however, always work to the advantage of the recipient of relief. 'The personal touch', as the Webbs pointed out, 'was Oliver Twist's grievance not his consolation.'[77] Local authorities were usually more concerned with keeping down the cost of relief than with increasing its effectiveness. Thus outdoor relief in cash was often preferred to indoor relief on financial as much as on humanitarian grounds. In London in 1862 a pauper in the workhouse cost the ratepayer 4s. 8d. a week as compared to 2s. 3d. for an outdoor pauper. Critics were swift to point out what some boards of guardians did not even attempt to deny, that the outdoor relief given was insufficient to maintain the recipient, who was forced to supplement the dole by honest or dishonest means.

Those who were sent to the workhouse were frequently unfortunates who could not care for themselves, and who had no one to look after them outside its walls. The sick, the aged, and orphaned or abandoned children constituted the largest proportion of the inmates. In order to keep down the costs, most boards of guardians had decided in favour of one large workhouse, in place of the smaller specialised institutions which some reformers had advocated. All types of pauper, sick, able-bodied, aged, mentally defective and orphan, were consigned to these 'general

[77] Webb, *English Local Government,* ix 965.

mixed' workhouses in which they were separated, with varying degrees of efficiency, by age and sex. Workhouse conditions varied according to the generosity and efficiency of the board of guardians and the ability and humanity of the master and matron. Thomas Archer found one in North-east London which he described as a clean, cheerful place with a light airy nursery, a well-equipped playground for the children, and a reading-room for the old men.[78] If few achieved this high standard, few perhaps sank to the level of the notorious Andover workhouse where in the mid-1840s it was alleged that the half-starved inmates gnawed at the rotting bones they had been given to crush as a work task. Most Victorian workhouses fell between the two extremes, giving their inmates accommodation in sanitary but bleak wards and food in the shape of a stodgy and frequently ill-cooked diet.

Much of the blame for the meanness of both outdoor and indoor relief has been laid at the door of the local authorities, the boards of guardians, who, it was alleged, guarded the rates more effectively than they guarded the poor. Given the failure to reform the rating system in 1834, however, some of this parsimony is explicable. Until 1865 each parish remained responsible for the cost of relieving its own paupers, and until 1861 a parish's contribution to the common expenses of the Union was assessed on the basis of its relief expenditure, not its rateable value, on its poverty rather than on its property. Parishes with large working-class populations found great difficulty in collecting poor rates in periods of trade depression, and thus were unable to meet the demands of the board of guardians for money. The guardians found their financial resources dwindling at a time when calls upon them were greatest.

The Union Chargeability Act of 1865 placed the whole cost of poor relief upon the Union rather than the parish, and thus redressed the inequality of burden between rich and poor parishes within the same Union. Inequalities between Unions remained, however, and guardians in poor areas like the East End of London had to husband their slender resources against periods of heavy demand. The small farmers and petty tradesmen who made

[78] T. Archer, *The Pauper, the Thief and the Convict* (1865).

up the majority of most boards of guardians were undoubtedly conventional in their attitude to the poor and unlikely to adopt imaginative and progressive schemes for dealing with poverty. Yet, in assessing their record, allowance must be made for the difficulties of their financial state.

One of the criticisms directed against the boards of guardians and the poor relief system which they administered was that the poor were being treated 'in a lump', given a meagre dole or confined in a general mixed workhouse with little or no attention paid to their special needs. Investigations of poverty in Victorian England were beginning to reveal its many-sided nature, and thus demand was increasing for more specialist treatment of different categories of pauper.

There was an early realisation of the special needs of the child pauper. Even before 1834, voices had been raised against the mingling of children with adult paupers, especially those of vicious or idle habits, in workhouses. After 1834, the Poor Law Commission, influenced by assistant commissioners like J. P. Kay who was a strong advocate of efficient education to raise workhouse children out of pauperism, impressed on boards of guardians the need to educate, if possible in separate institutions, the children in their workhouses. Although the attempt to persuade Unions to pool their resources to finance district schools for pauper children did not meet with great success, some more progressive boards of guardians, Leeds and Manchester for example, established industrial schools where pauper children could be lodged and educated.

By the 1860s, however, there was increasing criticism of these 'barrack schools' which, it was argued, were producing institution-bred pupils who were unable to cope with everyday life once they left the school. Some boards of guardians began to experiment with the Scots system of 'boarding out' children with working-class families, and the central authority gave its rather grudging approval to this mode of relief in 1870. Some twenty years later the Sheffield board of guardians developed the system of 'scattered homes' whereby the board took over a number of houses in various parts of the city and accommodated a small number of pauper children in each one under the care of a married couple appointed by the guardians. In this way it was hoped to re-create the conditions of family life and thus aid the child in a positive and constructive fashion.[79]

Another group for whom better treatment was demanded were the sick poor. Boards of guardians left their sick to be treated in their own homes by an ill-paid Union medical officer, or consigned more serious cases to the sick wards of the workhouse to be cared for by unskilled pauper nurses. As has been seen, protests by poor law medical officers against their treatment and that of their patients was given national publicity through organisations like the Poor Law Medical Officers' Association or the Workhouse Visiting Society and in the columns of the *Lancet*. The *Lancet*'s report on the state of the sick poor in London workhouses in 1865 shocked public opinion. An Association for the Improvement of the Conditions of the Sick in Workhouses, whose executive committee included such eminent Victorians as Lord Shaftesbury, Charles Dickens, Walter Bagehot and Thomas Hughes, was formed, and pressed the Poor Law Board to instigate further inquiries and order boards of guardians to improve the state of their workhouse infirmaries. 'Sickness and poverty are different things', proclaimed *The Times* in 1866. 'To confound them or to treat them alike is bad system or bad administration or a general confusion of ideas.'[80] In response to this pressure, the Poor Law Board issued a circular to boards of guardians advising them to provide better-equipped sick wards with properly trained nurses, and also appointed a Medical Inspector, Dr Edward Smith, with special responsibility for supervising the relief of the sick poor. In 1867 the Metropolitan Poor Act made provision for the establishment of separate asylums for the care of the sick,

[79] See S. and B. Webb, *English Poor Law Policy* (new ed., 1963) pp. 43–6, 104–15, 179–206; Rose, *The English Poor Law, 1780–1930*, pp. 178–91, 256–8; F. Duke, 'The Education of Pauper Children : Policy and Administration, 1834–1855', M.A. thesis (Manchester, 1968); A. M. Ross, 'J. P. Kay and the Training of Teachers for Poor Law Schools', *British Journal of Educational Studies* (1967).

[80] Association for Improvement of London Workhouses, *Opinions of the Press upon the Condition of the Sick Poor in London Workhouses* (1867), Manchester Central Reference Library, Pamphlets P.3056/5, p. 14.

insane or infirm poor in London, and also for the setting up of dispensaries to administer outdoor medical relief. Other large urban Unions also began to provide separate infirmaries for the sick poor, and in some cases to admit non-pauper patients, particularly those suffering from infectious diseases, to them. This development was aided by the Medical Relief Disqualification Act of 1885 which removed some of the stigma of pauperism from those who received only medical assistance from the poor law. The need for specialised treatment of the sick poor was gaining increasing recognition.[81]

It was of course easier for the central authority to accede to demands for separate and improved treatment of sick or child paupers, or of the aged or the mentally defective, since these all fell into the category of 'non-able-bodied' paupers for whom the rigours of the 1834 system were not intended. More difficulty was experienced with arguments for special treatment of the able-bodied pauper who, according to the 'principles of 1834', ought to be deterred from seeking relief and thus encouraged to fend for himself. Yet there was a growing recognition of the need to distinguish between the genuinely unemployed and the work-shy. Guardians in industrial areas, even if they sympathised with the aims of the New Poor Law, frequently objected to sending all able-bodied applicants for relief to the workhouse or setting them to task work, since this would involve mixing honest workmen put out of work through no fault of their own with the idle and feckless whose indolent habits they might contract.[82]

This problem was brought to a head by the Lancashire cotton famine of the early 1860s, in which thousands of factory operatives were thrown out of work. Independent, thrifty, members of co-operative and friendly societies and sometimes of trade unions and chapels, placing great store by the virtues of self-help and respectability, such men regarded both poor relief and private charity with contempt.

[81] Webb, *Poor Law Policy*, pp. 46–9, 115–23, 207–26; Rose, *The English Poor Law, 1780–1930*, pp. 171–8; O'Neill, op. cit.; Hodgkinson, *The Origins of the National Health Service*; Jeanne L. Brand, *Doctors and the State, 1870–1912* (1965) chap. 5.

[82] Rhodes Boyson, *The Ashworth Cotton Enterprise, 1818–1880* (1970) pp. 184, 188.

In recognition of the special needs of the Lancashire cotton worker, the Poor Law Board ordered local boards of guardians to be flexible with regard to restrictions on outdoor relief to able-bodied men. Committees were formed both inside and outside Lancashire to raise funds and distribute them to the distressed. Yet given the dislike of many workers both for the degradation of poor relief and the patronage of private charity, there was a feeling that these remedies were inadequate in such circumstances, and that government, both central and local, should intervene to create employment opportunities. The Public Works (Manufacturing Districts) Act of 1863 gave power to local authorities to apply for cheap loans from the Public Works Loan Commissioners and use the money to finance local improvements. Dr Henderson has shown, in his classic study of the cotton famine, that the Act 'failed to fulfil the sanguine hopes of its promoters as an answer to the unemployment problem'.[83] Nevertheless, it symbolised the failure of the nineteenth-century poor law to cope with the problem of large-scale industrial unemployment.

In the next decade the Local Government Board and its inspectorate attempted to reduce the amount of outdoor relief being granted by urging boards of guardians to enforce the regulations restricting outdoor relief more stringently. This crusade against outdoor relief made any use of the poor law system as a device to cope with unemployment even less possible. Deterred by the harshness and degradation of workhouse and labour tests, the unemployed sought relief for their condition from other sources.[84] This trend was given official recognition during the economic depression of the mid-1880s, when Joseph Chamberlain, the President of the Local Government Board, issued a circular urging local authorities to undertake public works as a means of relieving unemployment, and thus prevent the genuinely unemployed from having to submit to the humiliating process of applying for poor relief.

Yet despite its failure with regard to unemployment, the poor law system of the late nineteenth century was gradually moving towards greater specialisation in the treatment of those committed

[83] W. O. Henderson, *The Lancashire Cotton Famine, 1861–1865* (1934) p. 67.

[84] S. Pollard, *A History of Labour in Sheffield* (1959) pp. 182–4.

40

to its care. An indication of this can be found in the fact that expenditure on indoor relief rose by 113 per cent between 1871–2 and 1905–6, although the number of indoor paupers increased by only 76 per cent.[85] More specialised institutions were being built and greater classification was taking place within existing ones. It was no doubt with these trends in mind that Canon Barnett argued in 1883 that the poor law could be developed 'so as to make the life of England healthier and more restful'. In Barnett's view, outdoor relief to the aged could be replaced by old-age pensions, workhouses be turned into technical schools to provide trade training for inmates, and poor law medical services, both indoor and outdoor, be made available as of right to all comers.[86]

Under Barnett's scheme, the poor law would have become the basis of a modern system of social services. In fact, English welfare services were developed largely as a result of attempts to remove various classes of the poor from dependence on poor relief. The poor law stood condemned for two reasons. In the first place, large sections of the working class regarded it with fear and loathing. At the psychological level, 'less eligibility' had been all too successful. In the eyes of working people, anything controlled by the poor law authorities was automatically tainted with the shameful stigma of pauperism. In the second place, the Local Government Board and its officials did little to remove this taint. All too frequently they looked coldly on schemes to develop poor relief in a progressive and constructive fashion. As the Minority Report of the Royal Commission of 1905–9 pointed out, this official attitude condemned the poor law to the status of a residual service, a destitution authority, dealing with those who had fallen into pauperism, but unable because of this attitude to do anything to prevent the fall.

In the conditions of the late nineteenth century, with its increasing awareness of poverty as distinct from pauperism, and the growing demand for an attack upon it, the poor law was bound to become increasingly inadequate and even irrelevant.

[85] Royal Commission on the Poor Laws, *Report*, Part II, Cd 4499 (1909) p. 26.
[86] S. A. Barnett, 'Practicable Socialism', *Nineteenth Century*, XIII (1883).

Its controllers were unwilling to expand into new fields of social action, and even had they done so it is doubtful if the poor would have accepted them. Thus it is hardly surprising that other agencies became more important than the boards of guardians in dealing with various types of poverty. Urban school boards after 1870, and local education authorities after 1902, played a vital role in exposing and dealing with child poverty. School feeding and medical inspection developed out of the work of these bodies and not out of the poor law system. At the other end of the age spectrum, opinion was moving in favour of old-age pensions in some form to take the aged poor out of the sphere of the poor law. A Royal Commission on the Aged Poor had reported in 1895 in favour of improvement of poor law provisions for old people but had rejected the pensions idea. In 1899, however, the Government, under pressure of public opinion, was forced to appoint a Parliamentary Select Committee on the Aged Deserving Poor which reported in favour of a pension, albeit of a type which would have been little more than outdoor relief under another name. Such a scheme was unlikely to satisfy those who were by this time advocating state pensions of the type suggested by Charles Booth in his book *Old Age Pensions and the Aged Poor,* pensions of 7s. a week payable to all over the age of seventy out of national taxation.[87]

As far as the unemployed poor were concerned, the policy of the Chamberlain Circular, that of providing work for the unemployed, was continued both by local authorities and by some philanthropic bodies such as the Salvation Army. In 1904, with employment opportunities worsening, the Local Government Board encouraged the establishment of joint distress committees in London, composed of representatives of borough councils, boards of guardians and charitable organisations, to plan and co-ordinate schemes of work relief for the unemployed. The local committees examined applicants for relief, and attempted to distinguish the undeserving who were referred to the board of guardians from the genuinely unemployed who were given work

[87] C. Booth, *Old Age Pensions and the Aged Poor* (1899); Gilbert, *The Evolution of National Insurance in Great Britain,* chap. 4; D. Collins, 'The Introduction of Old Age Pensions in Great Britain', *Historical Journal,* VIII (1965).

which did not involve the deterrent aspects of the poor law labour test.

In 1905 the Conservative Government passed the Unemployed Workmen Act, requiring the establishment of similar distress committees in every large urban area in the country. As well as providing employment for those thought to be genuinely in need, the committees were also empowered to set up labour exchanges, keep unemployment registers, and assist the migration or emigration of unemployed workmen. This Act, as Professor Gilbert has shown, marks the culmination of attempts to deal with unemployment by means of work relief.[88] To those who still believed in less eligibility and the 'principles of 1834', it seemed to be a step fraught with danger. With poor relief costs and the numbers on outdoor relief increasing, there were fears in some minds that the evils of the Old Poor Law were being resurrected. One member of the House of Lords even foresaw the establishment of government workshops for the unemployed on the lines of the ill-fated *ateliers nationaux* in France after 1848.[89]

It was no doubt with the problems raised by this controversy in mind that the Conservative Government, in November 1905, announced the appointment of a Royal Commission on the Poor Laws and the Relief of Distress. Beatrice Webb suggested, somewhat maliciously, that its appointment was the result of the personalities of the President of the Local Government Board, Gerald Balfour, a philosopher 'who recognised the public advantage of a precise discrimination between opposing principles', and the new permanent head of the Poor Law Division of the Board, James Stewart Davy, 'an energetic man of affairs intent on reaction', who hoped that the Royal Commission would report in favour of the more stringent application of the 1834 Act, particularly with regard to the relief of the able-bodied.[90] More recent research has shown, however, that the Government were considering the appointment of a Royal Commission late

[88] Gilbert, *The Evolution of National Insurance in Great Britain*, p. 238. Chap. 5 of this work contains a detailed discussion of the developments leading up to the 1905 Act.

[89] The Earl of Wemyss. See Hansard, *Parliamentary Debates*, 4 Aug 1905, col. 240.

[90] Beatrice Webb, *Our Partnership* (1948) p. 317.

in 1904 at the same time as they were discussing the Unemployed Workmen Bill, the two being seen as complementary measures to deal with the deteriorating employment situation.[91]

Of the Royal Commission's twenty members, five were guardians of the poor and four top civil servants from the Local Government Board. Six, including Mrs Bosanquet, Octavia Hill and C. S. Loch, were members of the Charity Organisation Society. Charles Booth was appointed to the Commission, as was his former 'industrious apprentice', Beatrice Webb who, together with her husband, was engaged in research for their detailed and classic *History of the English Poor Law*. The Commission thus included a far more formidable body of expertise, both practical and theoretical, than its predecessor of 1832–4 had done. It also carried out a more detailed inquiry, visiting 200 Unions and 400 institutions, hearing 450 witnesses, and reading 900 statements of written evidence. Their inquiries took three years to complete, and filled forty-seven volumes. Yet despite this lengthy and careful investigation, it became obvious by 1907 that the Commission would not produce a united report. When the Commission finally reported in February 1909, a Minority Report, composed by Beatrice Webb and her husband, appeared. Its signatories were Mrs Webb herself, George Lansbury, the Poplar socialist, poor law guardian and borough councillor, Francis Chandler, trade unionist and former chairman of the Chorlton-on-Medlock (Manchester) board of guardians, and the Rev. Russell Wakefield, Dean of Norwich.

Despite the very considerable differences between the Majority and Minority Reports, there was perhaps more common ground between them than is often realised. Both were agreed in their condemnation of the existing system of poor relief. They criticised the failure of the central authority to impose any degree of uniformity in relief practice on local boards of guardians. At the local level the guardians were found to be doling out relief without making proper inquiries as to the needs of the case. The relieving officers who carried out their instructions were overworked and ill-trained. Despite increasing specialisation, too many

[91] J. Brown, 'The Appointment of the 1905 Poor Law Commission', *Bulletin of the Institute of Historical Research*, XLII (1969).

workhouses were still of the 'general mixed' type with all classes of pauper jumbled together in them. The wasteful overlapping of services where town councils and other bodies were taking on functions which were also the responsibility of boards of guardians was noted with displeasure.

Both reports, therefore, argued for the abolition of the boards of guardians and poor law unions established under the Act of 1834. The Majority Report envisaged their replacement by public assistance authorities in each borough or county, consisting partly of members of the local borough or county council and partly of co-opted members. These bodies would be responsible for taking major decisions on finance, the control of institutions, the appointment of officers and the like. Public assistance committees of the authority would hear applications for relief and make decisions as to the amount and nature of the relief to be granted. In addition to these public bodies, the Report also envisaged the establishment in each area of voluntary aid committees composed of leading organisers of local charities. These, it was hoped, would work in close co-operation with the public assistance authority, and thus achieve the organised intermingling of public and private relief which the Charity Organisation Society had been working for since the 1870s.

Although the Majority Report envisaged a radical restructuring of the relief system, Beatrice Webb and her fellow signatories of the Minority Report feared that it presented 'a new appearance while maintaining the old substance underneath'.[92] They felt that its emphasis was still upon remedial measures for alleviating destitution rather than upon preventative measures for abolishing it.

The important role given to private charity, working in conjunction with the public service as if they were 'parallel bars', seemed to confirm this. The Minority Report by contrast advocated the 'break-up of the poor law'. The boards of guardians were to be abolished and their functions divided up among the various committees of the borough and county councils. Thus the sick and aged poor would become the responsibility of the health committee, child paupers of the education committee and

[92] Webb, *Our Partnership,* p. 426.

so on. The system would be co-ordinated by a registrar of public assistance who would have power to investigate cases and levy a charge for services where the ability to pay existed.

But the most radical changes envisaged by the Minority Report were those for dealing with the unemployed, the 'able-bodied poor'. Unemployment, it argued, was a national not a local problem, and responsibility for it should be taken out of the hands of local authorities, whether boards of guardians or town councils. A new department of central government, a Ministry of Labour, should be established with powers to tackle unemployment through a whole gamut of measures – labour exchanges, training and retraining schemes, public works programmes to be put into operation in periods of cyclical depression, and detention colonies for those who were wilfully idle.[93] By an expert, bureaucratic attack upon the major causes of poverty, the Minority Report aimed at its abolition.

Yet for all the lengthy detail of its inquiries and the multiform proposals of its reports, the Royal Commission failed to initiate any major changes in the relief of poverty before 1914. One reason for this was undoubtedly the split within the Commission. This division was exacerbated when the Webbs, alarmed by the initially favourable reception accorded to the Majority Report, began their 'raging, tearing propaganda' for the break-up of the poor law as advocated by the Minority Report. This campaign of committee-forming, public speaking and writing did a great deal to publicise the ideas of the Minority Report. It appealed strongly to socially conscious young Edwardians and made a contribution to that 'atmosphere of hopeful debate' which J. B. Priestley has described as being characteristic of the Edwardian era.[94] Yet, as a device to persuade or compel those in power to act,

[93] The Webbs, like Charles Booth, retained certain moral judgements despite their empirical approach to social problems. They had no horror of bureaucratic compulsion. In a letter of 1911, Beatrice Webb talked of 'the element of compulsion and disciplinary supervision of the persons who are aided . . . it is no use letting the poor come and go as they think fit . . . destitution must be prevented and where necessary penalised as a public nuisance'. B. Webb to Georgina Meinertzhagen, March 1911, Passfield Papers.

[94] J. B. Priestley, *The Edwardians* (1970) p. 108. The campaign

it was, if anything, counter-productive. In abandoning the persuasion of the study and the dinner-table for the demands of the platform, the Webbs risked antagonising leading members of both the Government and the Opposition. 'I am not sure that your plan of knife to knife opposition is the best and that there is not here the opportunity for something of the persuasiveness of which you and Mr Webb are masters', Haldane's sister warned Beatrice Webb in 1909.[95]

Perhaps more serious was the effect of the Minority's campaign in driving the signatories and supporters of the Majority Report into the arms of the *status quo* party. Most of the progressive reforms which the Majority Report had advocated were completely lost sight of, whilst the ranks of those who opposed any change in the system were greatly strengthened. Boards of guardians in general strongly objected to their proposed dissolution and vented their wrath at their annual poor law conferences on the 'socialistic' schemes of the Webbs. Their opposition was supported by the officials of the Poor Law Division of the Local Government Board who in turn were backed by their political chief, John Burns, whose relationship with the Webbs was based on mutual distaste. In the face of such opposition, the divided camp of the poor law reformers stood little chance of success.

Yet even had the Royal Commission's Report been unanimous, it seems doubtful that 'it would have been invincible'.[96] By the time the Commission reported, the Liberal Government, apparently oblivious of its proceedings, was already embarked on its own programme of reforms to deal with various aspects of poverty. Rather than risk tackling the thorny problem of poor law reform,

---

to 'Break Up the Poor Law' is described in Beatrice Webb's second volume of autobiography *Our Partnership,* although the whole episode might usefully be subjected to further inquiry.

[95] E. S. Haldane to B. Webb, 1909, Passfield Papers, section II. 4.

[96] U. Cormack, *The Royal Commission on the Poor Laws 1905–9 and the Welfare State,* C. S. Loch Memorial Lecture (1953); reprinted in A. V. S. Lochhead, *A Reader in Social Administration* (1968) p. 90.

the Government's measures evaded it altogether by constructing new institutions totally separated from the poor law system.

As Professor Bentley Gilbert has shown, these measures fell into two groups. The early legislation, the Education (Provision of Meals) Act of 1906, the Education (Administrative Provisions) Act of 1907, and the Old Age Pensions Act of 1908, all concerned reforms which had long been under discussion inside and outside Parliament. It required only the political will to carry them out, a will which was sharpened by the Government's desire to conciliate the infant Labour Party and, after 1907, to check a run of by-election reverses. In the long run, however, old-age pensions, school meals and medical inspections owed more to the work and writings of people like Charles Booth and Margaret McMillan than to the reforming capacity of the Liberal Government.

It was after 1908, in Gilbert's view, that the Liberal Government pushed forward into dangerous and unknown territory, entering the 'untrodden fields' of sickness and unemployment. This push was spearheaded by two members of the Government, David Lloyd George and Winston Churchill, aided in Parliament, the civil service and the Press by a small number of young men like C. F. G. Masterman, Robert Morant, William Beveridge and W. J. Braithwaite who had been inspired, often at university or through the Settlement Movement, by the social ideals of the late nineteenth century. The weapon with which they aimed to conquer the new territory was that of compulsory insurance, supplemented in the case of unemployment by the establishment of labour exchanges.

In taking the state into the insurance field and in introducing the element of compulsion, the reformers were undoubtedly entering new territory. Thus, as has often been pointed out, they were forced to look to the example of Germany where a system of compulsory insurance against sickness, accident and old age based on the triple contribution of employee, employer and state had developed from the initial Sickness Insurance Act of 1883. 'It was from Germany that we who were privileged to be associated with the application of the principle to the United Kingdom found our first inspiration and it is with her experience before us that we feel confident of the future', wrote Lloyd George in

1912.[97] Lloyd George had been impressed by the German scheme whilst visiting that country in 1908, and sent Braithwaite to Germany late in 1910 to find out 'all about it'.[98] Yet Braithwaite himself admitted that whilst the example of Germany was followed in the principle of compulsion and of making the scheme national, the English reformers could not be said to have copied German legislation, which was imposed on a clear field, whilst in England it had to be superimposed on a great variety of existing organisations.[99] Friendly societies, trade unions and commercial insurance companies had already developed the idea of insurance against such misfortunes as sickness, accident, death and, in some cases, unemployment. They formed a powerful vested interest which Lloyd George, with consummate political skill, appeased by bringing them into the health insurance scheme in the role of approved societies through whom the financial benefits of the scheme would be paid.

In the matter of unemployment insurance, Beveridge argued that the plan put forward in Part II of the National Insurance Bill of 1911 owed little to Germany, where no such provision existed, but far more to the working models supplied by some English trade unions, and to the suggestions of the Reports of the Royal Commission on the Poor Laws which had advocated the establishment of labour exchanges and, in the case of the Majority, an insurance scheme, as remedies for unemployment.[100]

The insurance idea in fact had its roots deep in the ideals of self-help and independence which the Victorian era had nurtured. The notion of benefits as of right in return for contributions instead of the shameful dependence of poor relief or the patronising doles of private charity appealed to large sections of the English public. Lloyd George showed great political acumen in conciliating deeply suspicious vested interests such as the insur-

[97] Foreword to L. G. Chiozza Money, *Insurance versus Poverty* (1912) p. viii.
[98] H. N. Bunbury (ed.), *Lloyd George's Ambulance Wagon: Being the Memoirs of William J. Braithwaite, 1911–1912* (1957) p. 85.
[99] Ibid., p. 82.
[100] Beveridge, *Power and Influence*, p. 80.

ance societies and the medical profession.[101] His young assistants performed administrative miracles in drafting such complex legislation so rapidly, and then in putting its provisions into effect within two years of its passage. Yet the Insurance Act of 1911 was a political substitute for the thoroughgoing overhaul and realignment of the English welfare services envisaged by the Royal Commission on the Poor Laws, particularly by those who signed its Minority Report. Lloyd George recognised this. 'Insurance necessary temporary expedient', he wrote in a note to one of his civil servants in 1911. 'At no distant date hope State will acknowledge a full responsibility in the matter of making provision for sickness, breakdown and unemployment. It really does so now, through Poor Law, but conditions under which this system had hitherto worked have been so harsh and humiliating that working class pride revolts against accepting so degrading and doubtful a boon.'[102] For better or worse, however, this 'temporary expedient' was to become the foundation stone of the modern English welfare system.

It is of course difficult to assess the value of the Liberal reforms in terms of their effect on poverty before the outbreak of the First World War. The Old Age Pension Act, confined as it was to the very poor, since only those with an income of less than £21 a year received the full pension of 5s. a week, drastically reduced the numbers of old people in receipt of outdoor relief from the boards of guardians. It did little, however, to reduce the numbers in workhouses and other institutions, such aged inmates being largely incapable of caring for themselves even if given an independent source of income. The Insurance Act of 1911 was not brought into operation until 1913, and therefore could have had little impact on poverty or pauperism before 1914. Unemployment insurance was in any case confined at first to a few skilled trades, whose members were unlikely except in periods of

---

[101] See Gilbert, *The Evolution of National Insurance in Great Britain*, chaps. 4 and 6; Brand, *Doctors and the State*, chap. 11; J. H. Treble, 'The Attitudes of Friendly Societies towards the Movement in Great Britain for State Pensions, 1878–1908', *International Review of Social History*, xv (1970).

[102] W. H. B. Court, *British Economic History, 1870–1914: Commentary and Documents* (1965) p. 413.

extreme distress to come on the poor law. The health insurance sickness benefit of 10s. a week alleviated to some extent the disaster which the illness of the bread-winner spelt for a poor family. But the medical benefits of the system were severely limited since they were confined to free G.P. treatment for the insured person only, and thus did nothing to improve the health of the wives and children of the poor. The fall in the numbers on poor relief between 1911 and 1914 owed more to the economic boom of the immediate pre-war period than it did to welfare legislation.

Despite the fall in the numbers on poor relief, the researches of A. L. Bowley and of Seebohm Rowntree in 1912 and 1913 revealed the continued existence of extensive poverty.[103] Bowley in 1911 estimated that 32 per cent of the adult male labour force earned less than 25s. a week, whilst in the same year Rowntree argued that the minimum cost of rent, food and clothing for a family of five was 21s.[104] Despite having been condemned by the Royal Commission's Report of 1909, and seriously undermined by the welfare legislation of the Liberal Government in the administration of which it was given no part, the poor law system remained little amended in 1914. Knowledge of poverty had increased enormously since the passage of the Act of 1834. Attitudes to poverty were changing and the principles of 1834 were being shown up as outdated and irrelevant. Yet the power or the will to tackle the problems of poverty had not, it seemed, kept pace with the change in knowledge or in attitudes. R. H. Tawney pointed to this in his inaugural lecture as director of the Ratan Tata Foundation, a body founded 'to promote the study and further the knowledge of methods of preventing and relieving poverty and destitution'.

Whilst progress was undoubtedly retarded in the nineteenth century through the contempt of our grandfathers for economic investigation [he remarked], there seems some danger that it may be paralysed in the twentieth through a supersti-

[103] Bowley and Burnett-Hurst, *Livelihood and Poverty*; B. S. Rowntree, *How the Labourer Lives* (1913).
[104] P. Snowden, *The Living Wage* (1912) pp. 29, 39.

tious reverence for accumulated facts; and I should be very sorry to be thought to suppose that the future welfare of mankind depended principally upon the multiplication of sociologists. There are, it is true, a considerable number of matters where practical action is delayed by the absence of sufficient knowledge. There are more perhaps where our knowledge is sufficient to occupy us for the next twenty years, and where the continuance of social evils is not due to the fact that we do not know what is right, but to the fact that we prefer to continue doing what is wrong. Those who have the power to remove them have not the will, and those who have the will have not, as yet, the power.[105]

[105] Tawney, *Poverty as an Industrial Problem*, p. 9. See also J. H. Winter, 'R. H. Tawney's Early Political Thought', *Past and Present* (1970).

Appendices

Appendix A

Mean Number[a] of Paupers Relieved, 1850–1914, in England and Wales

Year ending Lady Day[b]	Indoor paupers		Outdoor paupers		Total	
	Mean number	% of population	Mean number	% of population	Mean number	% of population
1850	123,004	0·77	885,696	5·0	1,008,700	5·7
1855	121,400	0·65	776,286	4·2	897,686	4·8
1860	113,507	0·58	731,126	3·7	844,633	4·3
1865	131,312	0·63	820,586	3·9	951,898	4·5
1870	156,800	0·71	876,000	3·9	1,032,800	4·6
1875	146,800	0·62	654,114	2·8	800,914	3·4
1880	180,817	0·71	627,213	2·5	808,030	3·2
1885	183,820	0·68	585,118	2·2	768,938	2·9
1890	187,921	0·66	587,296	2·1	775,217	2·7
1895	208,746	0·69	588,167	2·0	796,913	2·7
1900	215,377	0·68	577,122	1·8	792,499	2·5
1910	275,075[c]	0·78	539,642[c]	1·5	916,377	2·6
1914	254,644[c]	0·69	387,208[c]	1·0	748,019	2·0

[a] Mean of number relieved on 1 January of that year and 1 July of preceding year.
[b] 25 March.
[c] Does not include casuals and insane paupers.

Source: Local Government Board, *31st Annual Report* (1901–2). Appendix E, p. 312.

Appendix B

Pauperism in England and Wales, Scotland and Ireland, 1850–1908
(average daily numbers of paupers of all classes relieved
per 1,000 of population)

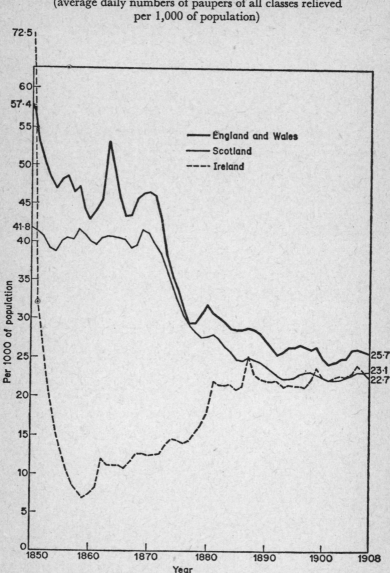

Source: Local Government Board, *Statistical Memoranda on Public Health
and Social Conditions*, section 4, Cd 4671 (1909).

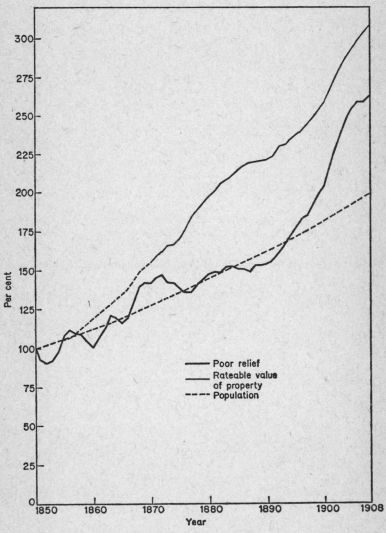

Appendix C

Cost of Poor Relief in Relation to Rateable Property and Population, England and Wales

(cost of relief, rateable value and population in 1850=100; figures for subsequent years in percentages of 1850 figures)

Source: see Appendix B.

Bibliography

THERE are a large number of contemporary works dealing with poverty and its allied problems in the nineteenth century. These range from full-blown treatises to pamphlets and articles in periodicals. To list even those known to the author would be well beyond the scope of this bibliography, which will deal only with the best known and most influential of them. Those who wish to pursue their researches beyond this would be well advised to consult the *Journals of the Royal Statistical Society* and the *Transactions of the National Association for the Promotion of Social Science*. General periodicals such as the *Nineteenth Century*, the *Quarterly Review* or *Macmillan's Magazine* also contain some articles of interest on poverty and other social problems.

Recent work on poverty and the poor law system in the nineteenth century is less extensive than is sometimes assumed. A good deal of research remains entombed in unpublished M.A. and Ph.D. theses. Those interested in the development of poor relief in a particular area should inquire after the existence of any such theses, and also consult the publications of local historical societies.

The classic work on the development of the poor law in this period is of course Sidney and Beatrice Webb, *English Poor Law History*, part 2 : *The Last Hundred Years*, which forms vols VIII and IX of their massive *English Local Government* (1929; reissued 1963). This can be usefully supplemented by the same authors' *English Poor Law Policy* (1910; reissued 1963). The latter volume discusses the policies of the central authorities responsible for the poor law in the nineteenth century, the Poor Law Commission (1834–47), the Poor Law Board (1847–71) and the Local Government Board (1871–1919), with reference to each category of pauper, the able-bodied, the sick, children, the aged and so on. When consulting the Webbs, the student must constantly bear in mind the active role which they played in the campaign for poor law reform, and their decided views on the subject as stated in the Minority Report of the Royal Commission of 1905–9.

Other works dealing with aspects of poverty, the poor law, social policy and research between 1834 and 1914 are as follows :

Thomas Archer, *The Pauper, the Thief and the Convict* (1865). Investigations into the life of the London poor and poor law institutions.

H. L. Beales, *The Making of Social Policy in the Nineteenth Century*, Hobhouse Memorial Lecture (1946). Discusses the development of social investigation in the face of *laissez-faire* attitudes.

——, 'The New Poor Law', *History*, xv (1931). Beautifully written, brief account of the thinking behind the 1834 Act.

Lady Florence Bell, *At the Works* (1907). Booth and Rowntree-style survey of Middlesbrough.

W. Beveridge, *Unemployment: A Problem of Industry* (1909). Analysis and definition of various types of unemployment. Developed idea of labour exchanges and unemployment insurance.

Charles Booth, *Life and Labour of the People in London*, 17 vols (1902–4).

A. L. Bowley and A. R. Burnett-Hurst, *Livelihood and Poverty* (1915). The most expert use of the social survey before 1914. Based on a study of Reading, Warrington, Northampton and Stanley (Co. Durham) in 1912–13.

J. L. Brand, *Doctors and the State: The British Medical Profession and Government Action in Public Health, 1870–1912* (1965). Useful chapters on poor law medical officers and on the reaction of the medical profession to the Royal Commission of 1905–9 and the Health Insurance Act of 1911.

Asa Briggs, *Social Thought and Social Action: A study of the Work of Seebohm Rowntree, 1871–1954* (1961). Chap. 2 contains an account of the making of the 1899 survey.

John Brown, 'Charles Booth and the Labour Colonies, 1889–1905', *Economic History Review*, xxi (1968). Shows how Booth's suggestion of labour colonies as a means of removing a section of the poor from the labour market revealed both the inadequacy of his analysis of unemployment and also certain moralistic attitudes in his scientific approach.

——, 'The Appointment of the 1905 Poor Law Commission', *Bulletin of the Institute of Historical Research*, xlii (1969). Challenges the Webbian view of the establishment of the Commission.

——, 'Social Judgements and Social Policy', *Economic History Review*, xxiv (1971). Debates with Trevor Lummis (see below)

57

the question as to whether Booth and other social investigators were moralists or empiricists.

M. Bruce, *The Coming of the Welfare State* (1961). Useful, if rather curiously organised, textbook on the development of social welfare from the eighteenth century to the present day.

Sir H. N. Bunbury (ed.), *Lloyd George's Ambulance Wagon: Being the Memoirs of W. J. Braithwaite, 1911–1912* (1957). Lively personal account of the drafting and passage of the 1911 Insurance Act. Critical introduction by R. M. Titmuss.

J. D. Burnett, *Plenty and Want: A Social History of Diet in England* (1966). Information on diets of the poorer classes.

D. Collins, 'The Introduction of Old Age Pensions in Great Britain', *Historical Journal*, viii (1965).

U. Cormack, *The Royal Commission on the Poor Laws 1905–9 and the Welfare State*, C. S. Loch Memorial Lecture (1953); reprinted in A. V. S. Lochhead, *A Reader in Social Administration* (1968). Stimulating defence of the Majority Report in face of the Minority Report's propagandists.

W. H. B. Court, *British Economic History, 1870–1914: Commentary and Documents*. Chaps. 6–8 contain excellent selection of source material relating to wages, living standards and poverty.

Maude Davies, *Life in an English Village* [Corsley, Wilts.] (1909). One of the first social surveys of a rural community. The author was a student at the London School of Economics, and was encouraged by the Webbs to carry out the investigation in 1905.

N. C. Edsall, *The Anti-Poor Law Movement, 1834–44* (1971). A detailed study of the resistance to the attempt to impose the Poor Law Amendment Act.

A. Fried and R. Elman, *Charles Booth's London* (1969). Selections from the 17 vols of *Life and Labour*. Useful, but no substitute for forays into the original.

B. B. Gilbert, *The Evolution of National Insurance in Great Britain: The Origins of the Welfare State* (1966). Excellent, scholarly account of attitudes to, and discussion of, poverty from the 1880s, leading up to the Liberal reforms of 1906–14. Comprehensive bibliography.

P. H. J. H. Gosden, *The Friendly Societies in England, 1815–75* (1961). Traces these important agencies of working-class thrift from their origins to the Act of 1875.

R. M. Gutchen, 'Local Improvements and Centralisation in Nineteenth Century England', *Historical journal*, iv (1961).

B. Harrison, 'Philanthropy and the Victorians', *Victorian Studies*, IX (1965–6).

W. O. Henderson, *The Lancashire Cotton Famine, 1861–1865* (1934). Standard work on this important episode for the history of Victorian poor relief.

E. P. Hennock, 'Finance and Politics in Urban Local Government, 1835–1900', *Historical Journal*, VI (1963).

R. Hodgkinson, *The Origins of the National Health Service: The Medical Services of the New Poor Law, 1834–71* (1967). Detailed account of the development of medical relief and of the important role played by poor law medical officers.

——, 'Social Medicine and the Growth of Statistical Information', in F. N. L. Poynter (ed.), *Medicine and Science in the 1860s* (1970). Excellent discussion of the early development of statistical approaches to social investigation.

J. R. T. Hughes, 'Henry Mayhew's London', *Journal of Economic History*, XXIX (1969).

P. d'A. Jones, *The Christian Socialist Revival, 1877–1914* (1968). Discusses the stirrings of social conscience among Churchmen in the late nineteenth century and its effects.

R. Lambert, *Sir John Simon, 1816–1904, and English Social Administration* (1963). Important, scholarly biography which does much to reverse the conventional view of mid-Victorian quietism in social reform.

T. Lummis, 'Charles Booth : Moralist or Social Scientist?', *Economic History Review*, XXIV (1971).

H. M. Lynd, *England in the 1880s: Toward a Social Basis for Freedom* (1945). Detailed account of a crucial decade in the development of social policy.

N. McCord, 'The Implementation of the 1834 Poor Law Amendment Act on Tyneside', *International Review of Social History*, XIV (1969). Shows that in its early years the Act worked reasonably well in this area.

O. R. McGregor, 'Social Research and Social Policy in the Nineteenth Century', *British Journal of Sociology*, VIII (1957). Important discussion of mid-Victorian developments in social investigation and planning.

T. Mackay, *A History of the English Poor Law*, vol. III : *1834–98* (1904). Supplementary volume to Sir George Nicholl's two-volume history. Interesting for its steadfast adherence to the 'principles of 1834'.

J. M. Mackintosh, *Trends of Opinion about the Public Health,*

1901–51 (1953). Early chapters deal with the development of personal health services in response to the growing concern about the physical state of the nation, and with the Insurance Act of 1911.

T. H. Marshall, *Social Policy* (1965). Discussion of modern British social policy with historical chapters by way of introduction. Valuable brief analysis of thinking behind social reform.

L. Masterman, *C. F. G. Masterman* (1939). Consists largely of extracts from Masterman's diaries.

H. Mayhew, *London Labour and the London Poor*, 4 vols (1851–62; reissued 1967). Well worth dipping into rather than relying on the numerous editions of extracts from Mayhew.

S. Mencher, *Poor Law to Poverty Programme: Economic Security Policy in Britain and the United States* (1967). Comparative study of ideas underlying welfare policy in Britain and the United States from the seventeenth century to the present day.

E. Midwinter, *Social Administration in Lancashire, 1830–1860* (1969). Chap. 2 deals with the introduction and administration of the New Poor Law in the county.

C. L. Mowat, *The Charity Organisation Society, 1869–1913* (1961). Useful brief study by a descendant of the society's influential secretary, C. S. Loch. A full-scale study is, however, much needed.

——, 'The Approach to the Welfare State in Great Britain', *American Historical Review*, LVIII (1952–3).

J. E. O'Neill, 'Finding a Policy for the Sick Poor', *Victorian Studies*, VII (1963–4).

D. Owen, *English Philanthropy, 1660–1960* (1965). Valuable discussions of Victorian charities, the C.O.S. and the Royal Commission of 1905–9.

H. Pelling, 'State Intervention and Social Legislation in Britain before 1914', *Historical Journal*, x (1967). Review article of B. B. Gilbert's and J. L. Brand's books.

——, *Popular Politics and Society in Late Victorian England* (1968). Chap. 1 discusses reaction of working-class voter to social welfare legislation.

S. Pollard, *A History of Labour in Sheffield* (1959). Valuable research on standard of living of working classes in this city and also on measures to deal with unemployment.

M. S. Pember Reeves, *Round About a Pound a Week*, 2nd ed. (1914). Research into life on the poverty line in London by a member of the Fabian Women's Group.

M. Richter, *The Politics of Conscience: T. H. Green and His Age* (1964). Detailed study of the life and thought of the mid-nineteenth-century Oxford philosopher whose notion of 'positive freedom' powerfully influenced late nineteenth-century social thought.

D. Roberts, *Victorian Origins of the British Welfare State* (1960). Discusses the development of Victorian social administration, particularly of the inspectorate, in various fields.

B. Rodgers, 'The Social Science Association, 1857–86', *Manchester School*, xx (1952). The only modern study of this important body.

M. E. Rose, *The English Poor Law, 1780–1930* (1971). Collection of extracts from published documents on poor relief with brief commentary.

——, 'The Allowance System under the New Poor Law', *Economic History Review*, xix (1966). Discusses extent of survival of practice of relief in aid of earnings despite strictures of the central authority.

B. S. Rowntree, *Poverty: A Study of Town Life* (1901). More manageable and more advanced study of poverty than Booth's.

——, *How the Labourer Lives* (1913). Details of living standards of agricultural labourers in various parts of country.

Royal Commission on the Poor Laws, *Report* (1834). Largely the work of Nassau Senior and Edwin Chadwick. Highlights the alleged evils of the Old Poor Law, and puts forward detailed recommendations for reform. 'That brilliant, influential and wildly unhistorical piece of special pleading', as R. H. Tawney described it.

Royal Commission on the Poor Laws and the Relief of Distress, *Majority and Minority Reports* (1909). Spells out the failure of the 1834 system. Between the Report of 1834 and those of 1909 lie a mass of parliamentary inquiries into the poor law and allied subjects. For a list of these, consult the indexes to *Parliamentary Papers*.

K. de Schweinitz, *England's Road to Social Security* (1943). Brief but useful survey of growth of British social welfare.

B. Semmel, *Imperialism and Social Reform* (1960).

M. B. Simey, *Charitable Effort in Liverpool in the Nineteenth Century* (1951). Discussion of development of philanthropic effort in a rapidly growing urban community.

T. S. and M. B. Simey, *Charles Booth, Social Scientist* (1960). Scholarly life which discusses the social surveys in detail.

E. P. Thompson, 'The Political Education of Henry Mayhew', *Victorian Studies,* xi (1967–8).

——, and Eileen Yeo (eds), *The Unknown Mayhew* (1971). Extracts from Mayhew's *Morning Chronicle* articles with important introductory essays putting forward the case for Mayhew as a serious social scientist.

Victorian Society, *The Victorian Poor: Fourth Conference Report* (1966). Publication of papers by E. P. Thompson, J. D. Burnett, A. Armstrong, H. J. Dyos, J. Tobias and Helen Meller on various aspects of mid-Victorian poverty.

Beatrice Webb, *My Apprenticeship* (1926); *Our Partnership* (1948). Two volumes of autobiography containing lively accounts of the author's training in social work under Charles Booth and her experience as a member of the Royal Commission of 1905–9.

A. S. Wohl, 'The Bitter Cry of Outcast London', *International Review of Social History,* xiii (1968).

K. Woodroofe, *From Charity to Social Work* (1962). Comparative study of development of social casework in Britain and United States. Early chapters discuss the role of the C.O.S. in this.

A. F. Young and E. T. Ashton, *British Social Work in the Nineteenth Century* (1956). Ranges over a wide area of social reform and reformers.

Index

64